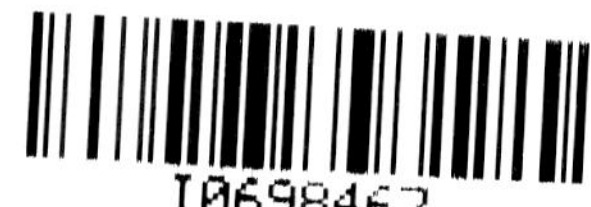

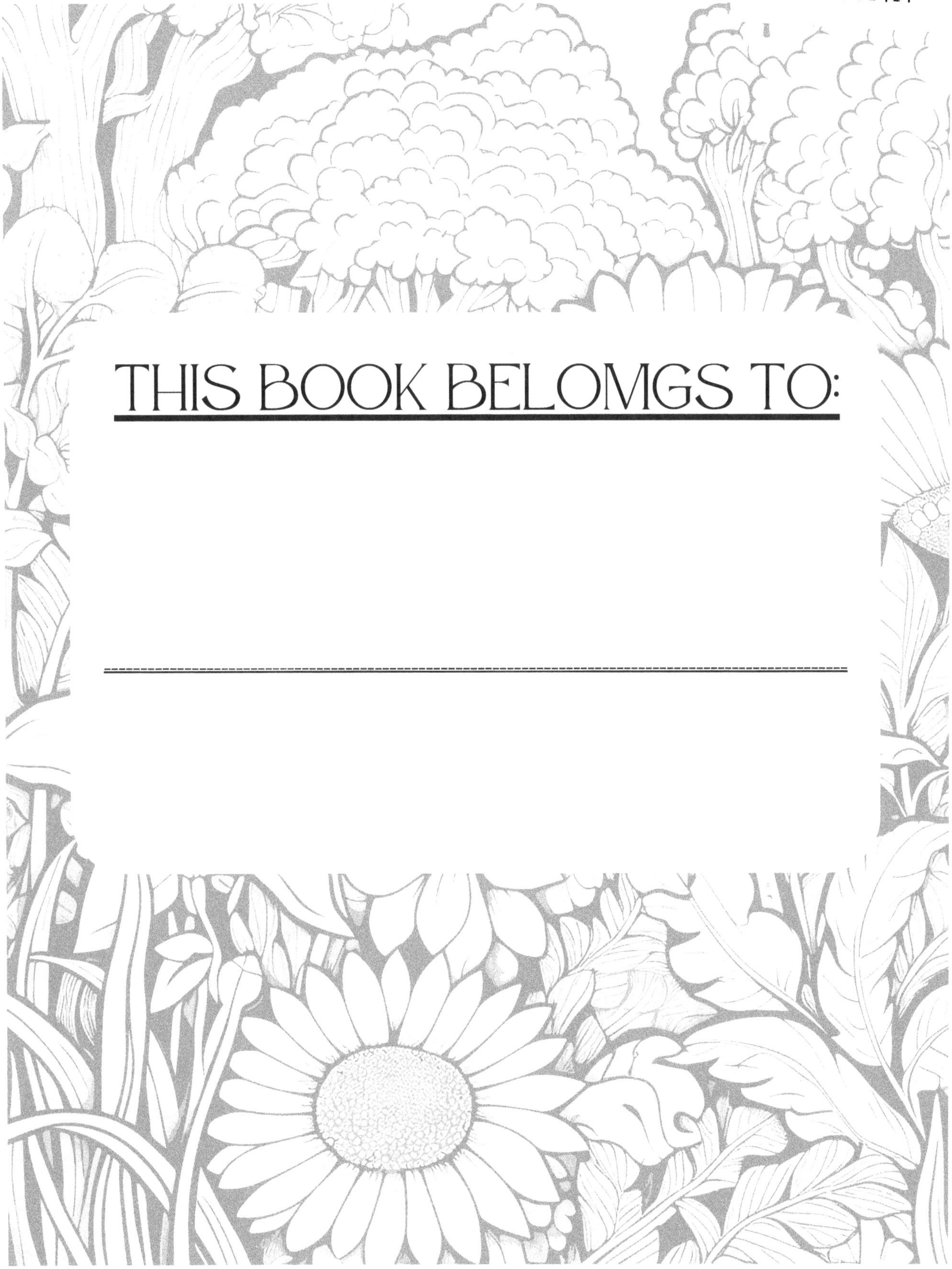

THIS BOOK BELOMGS TO:

COLOR TEST PAGE

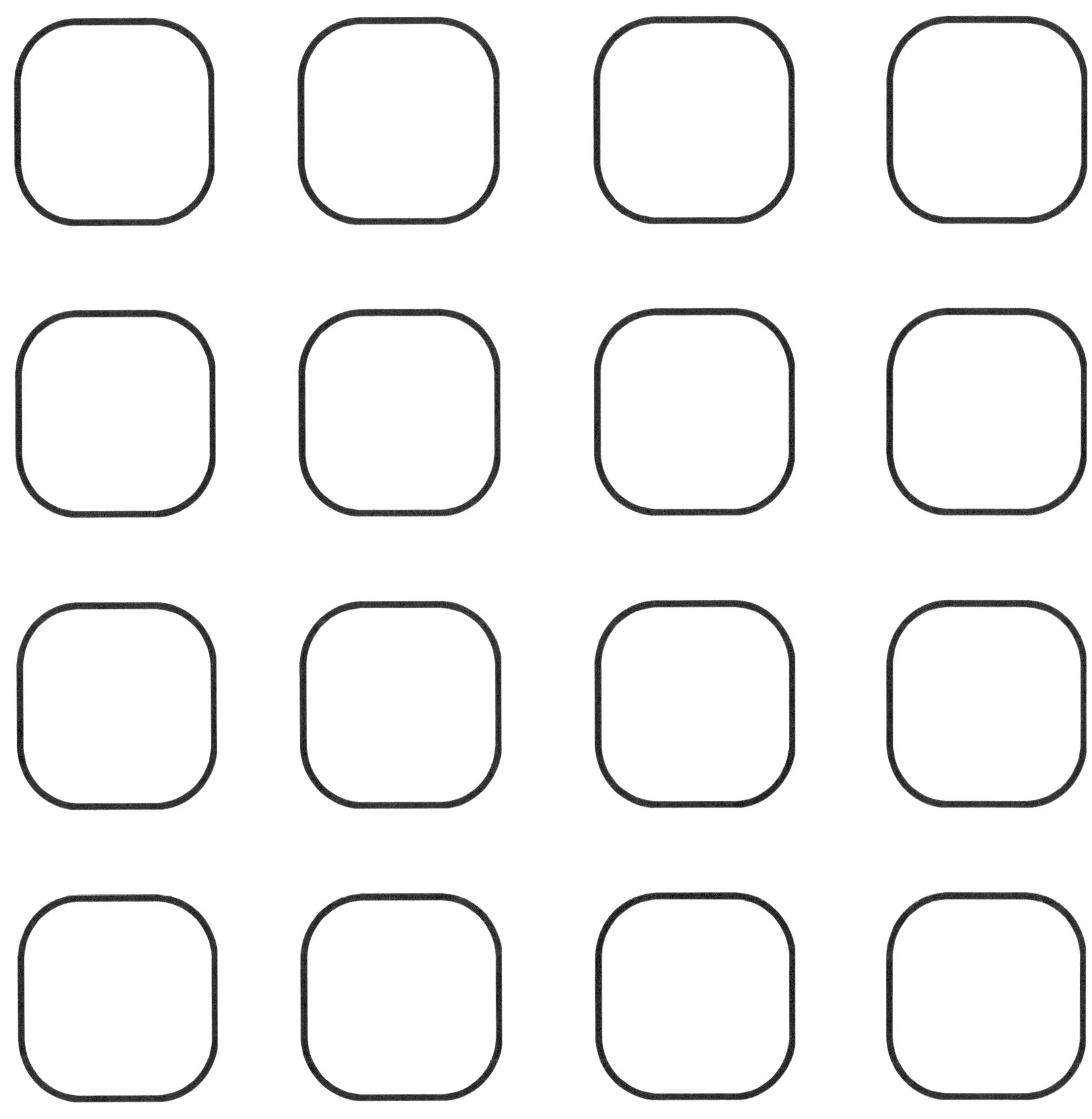

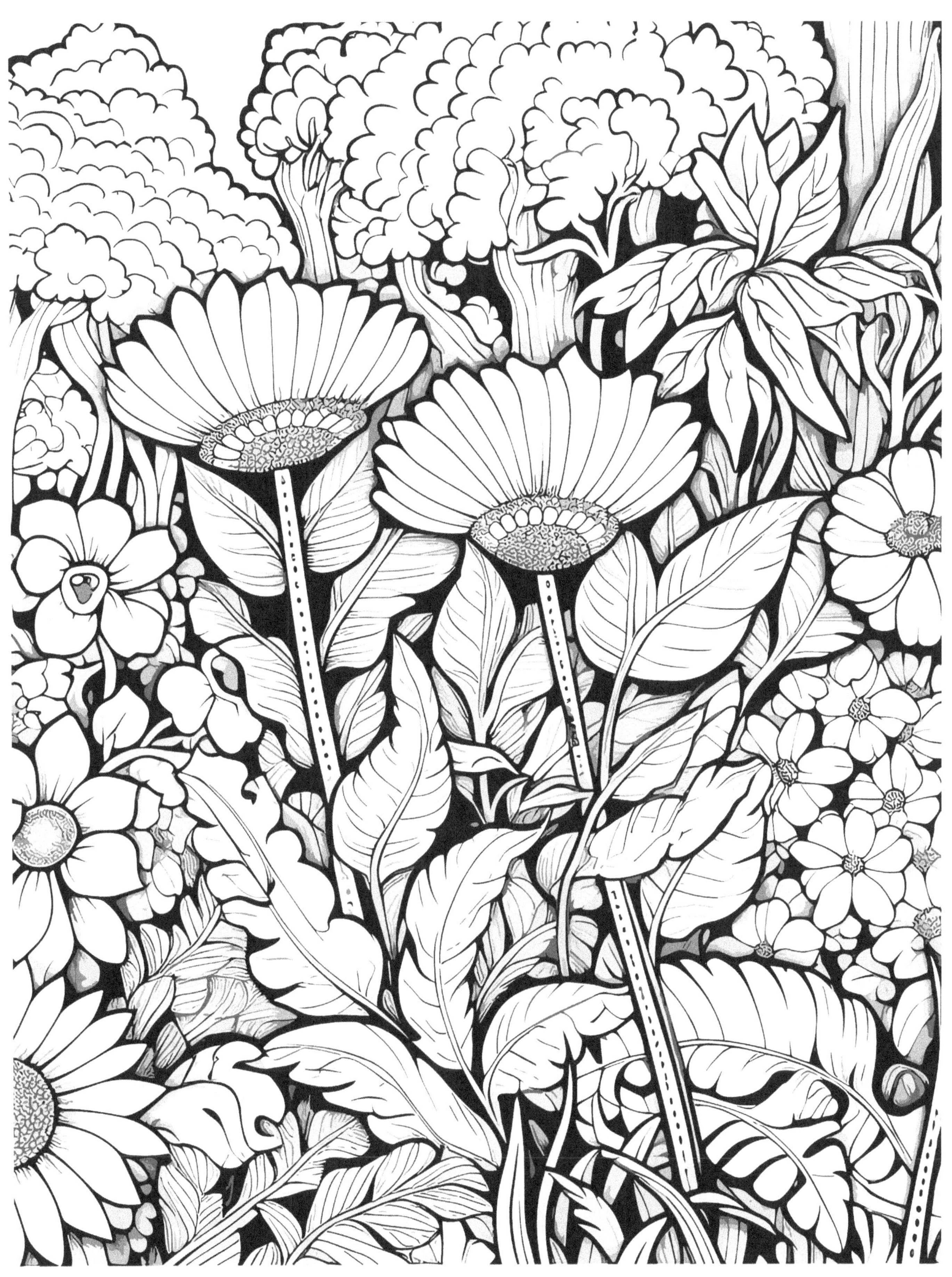

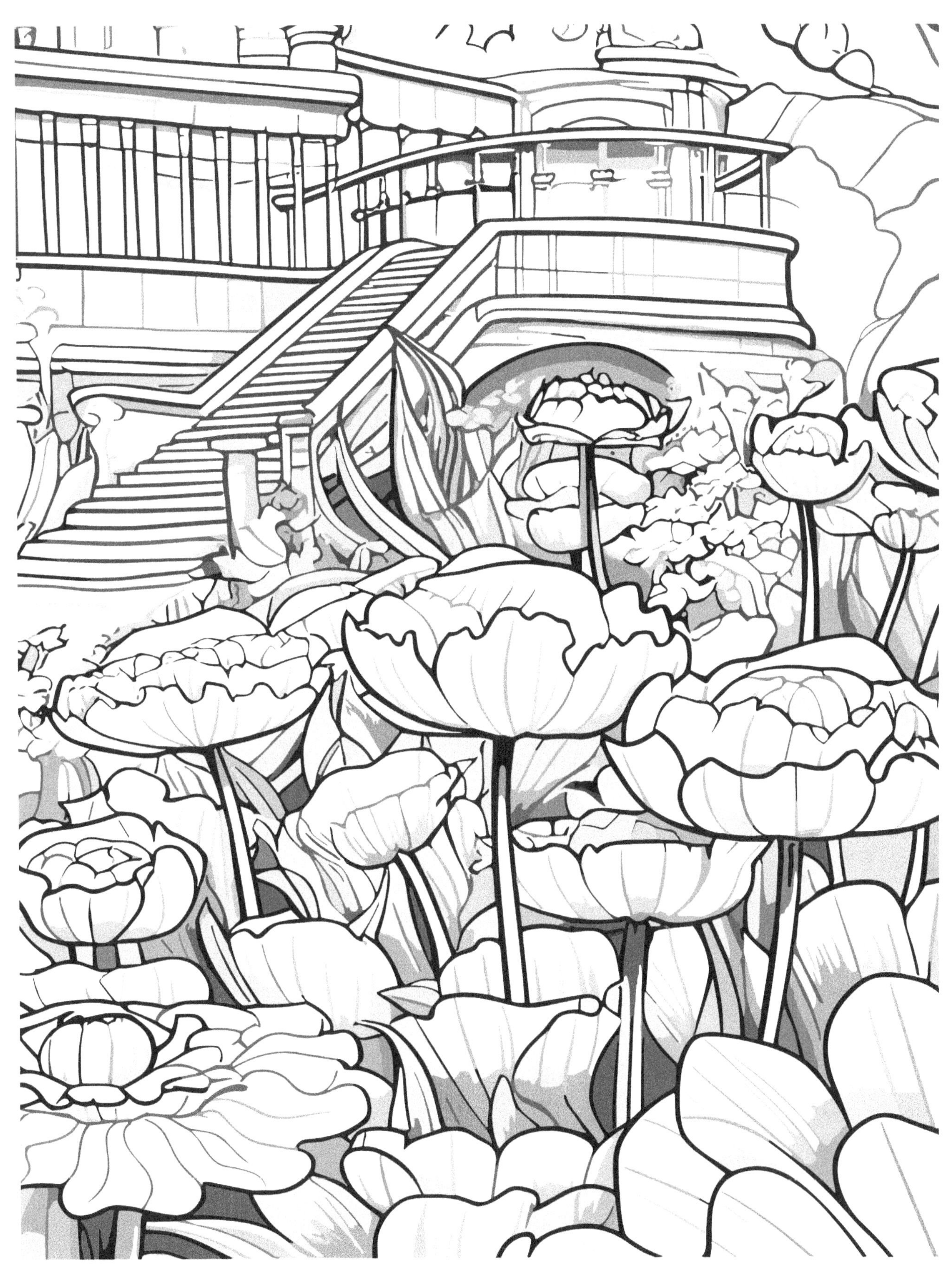

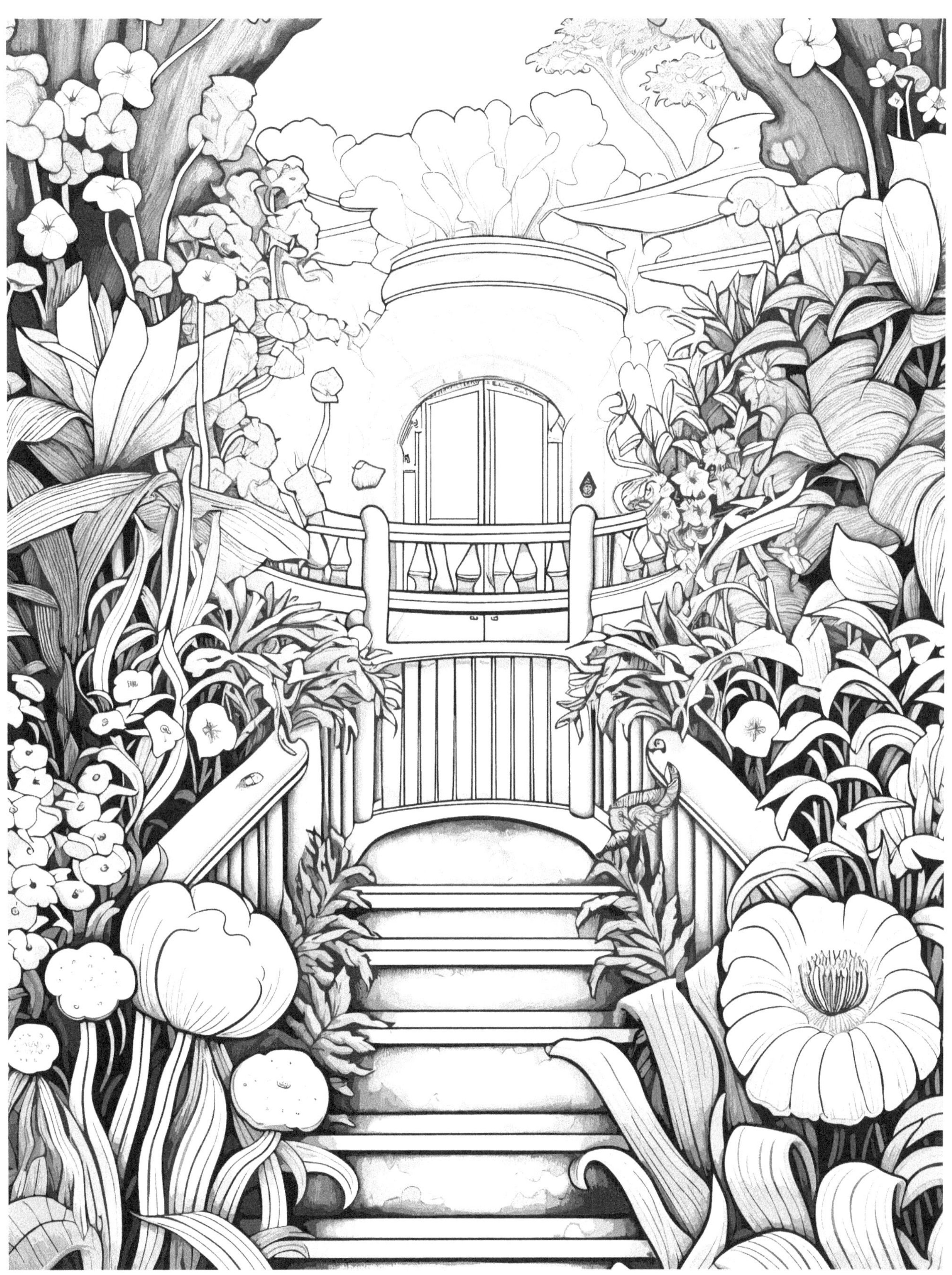

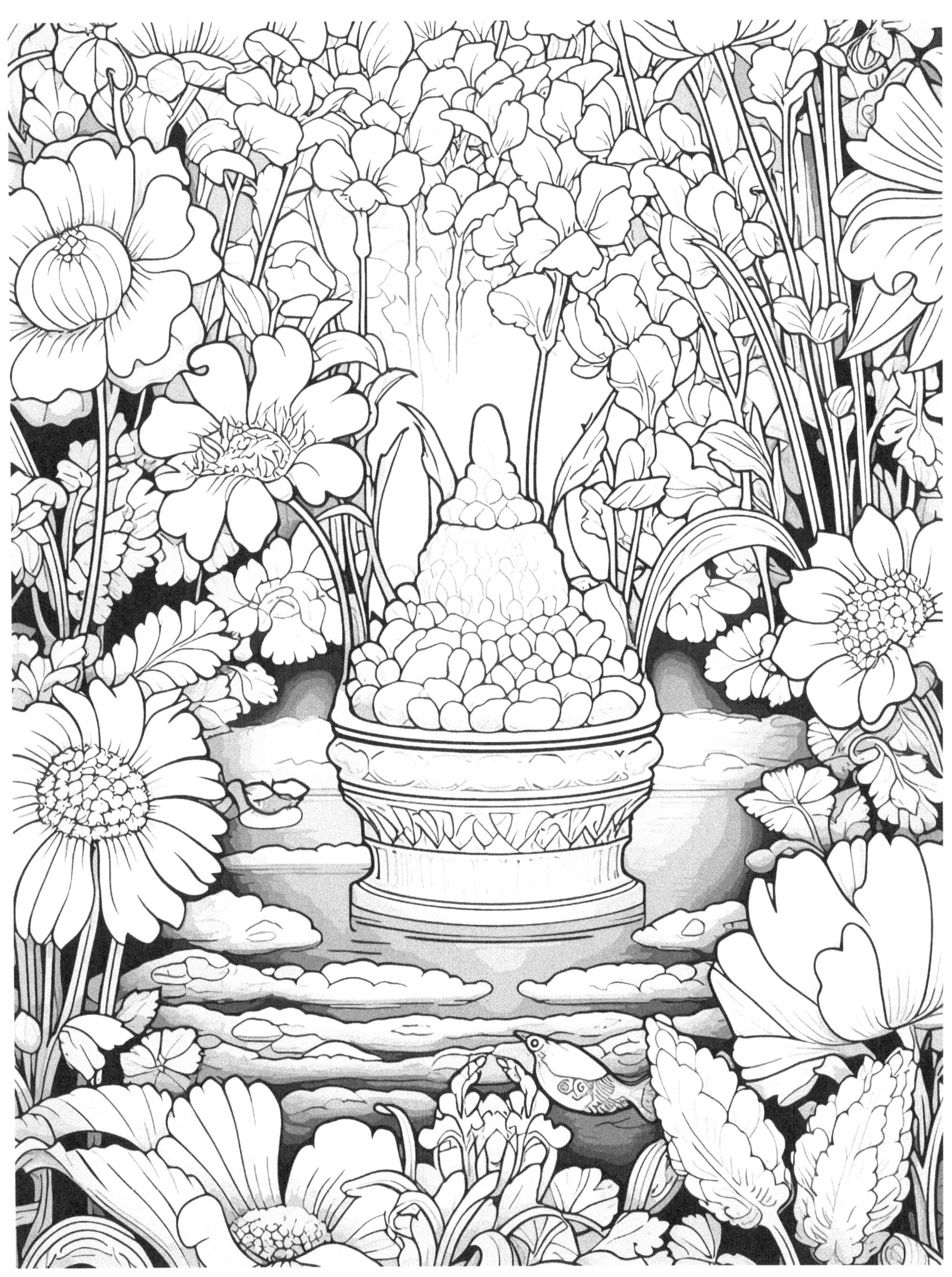

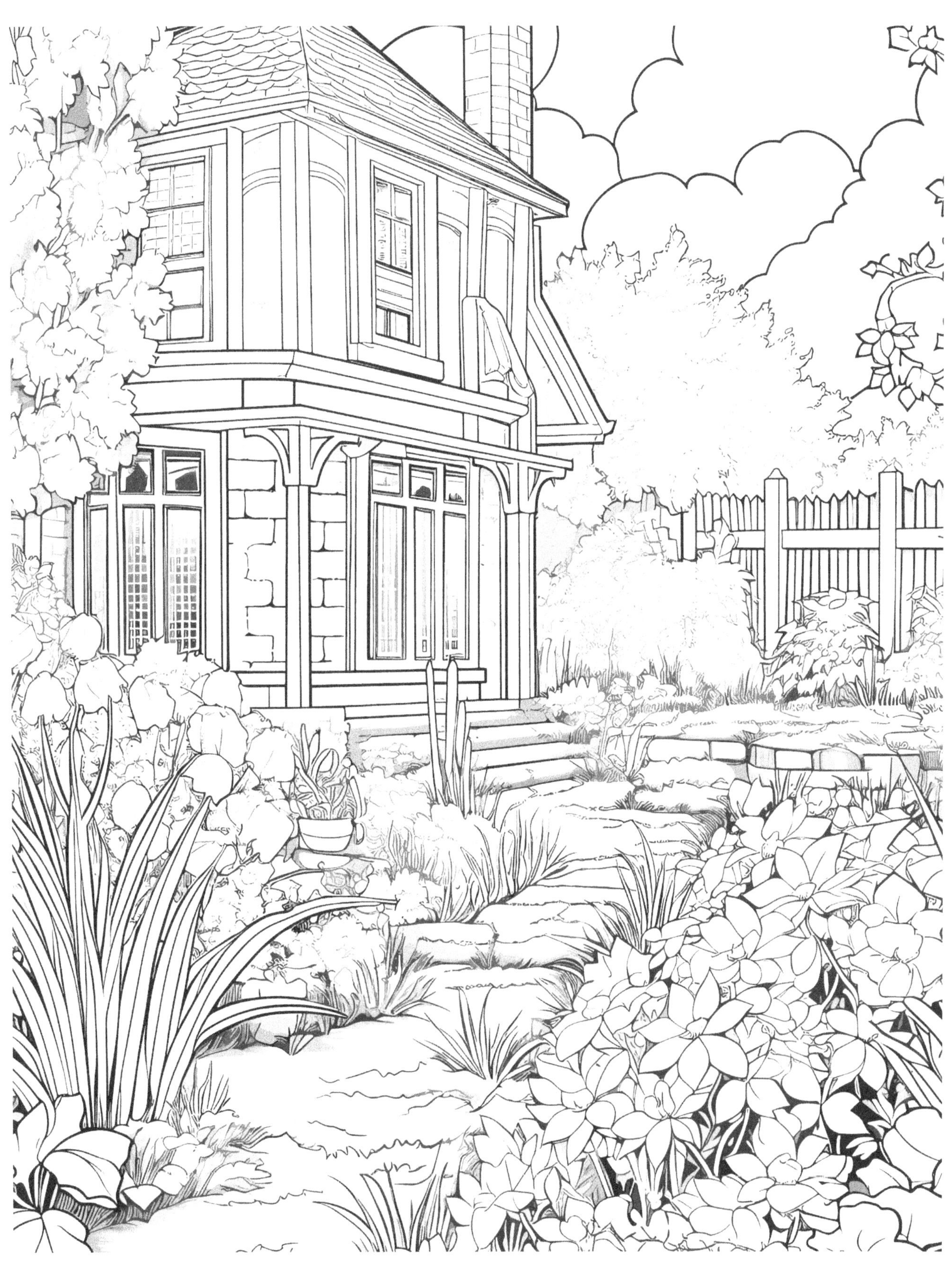

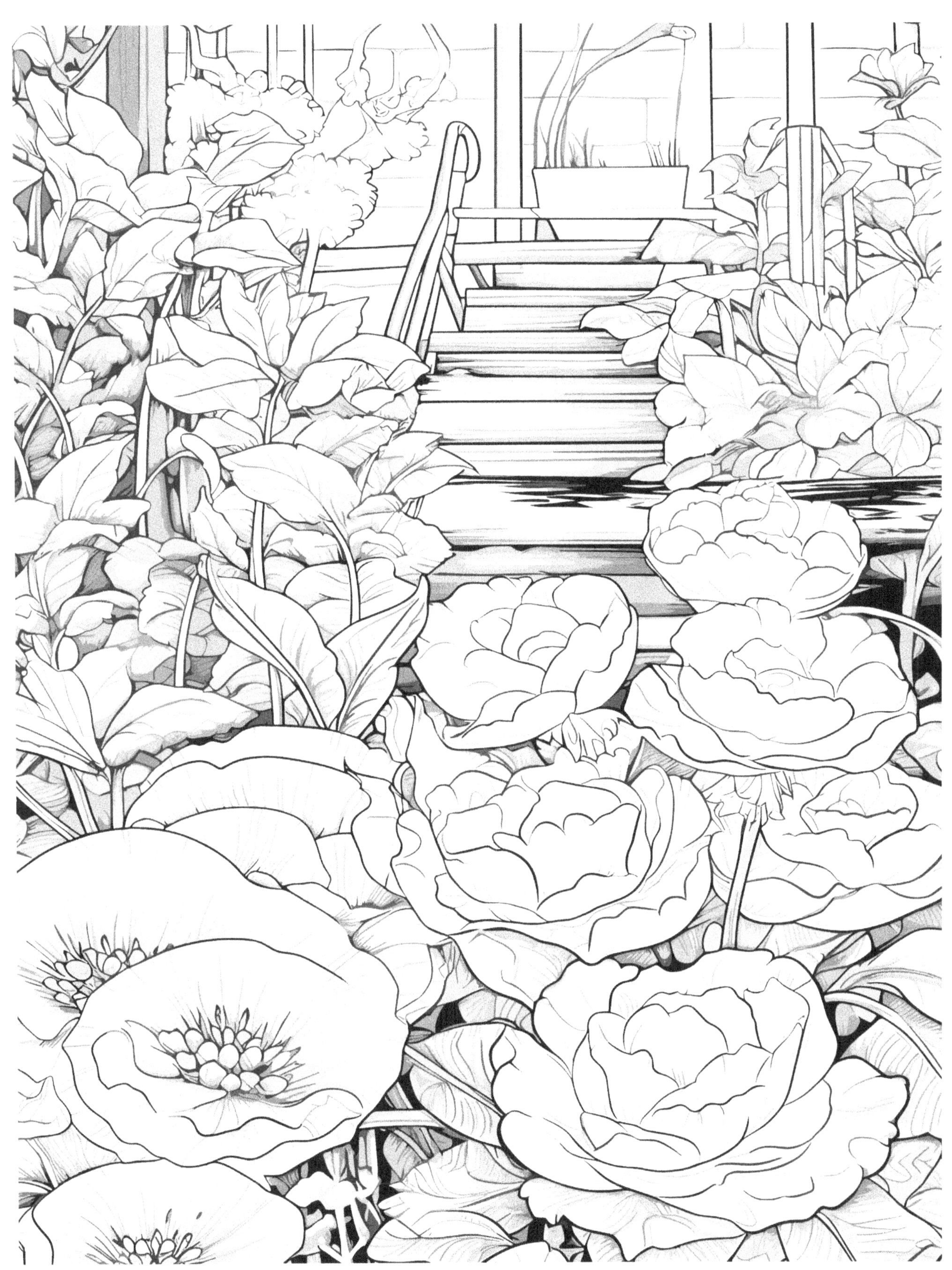

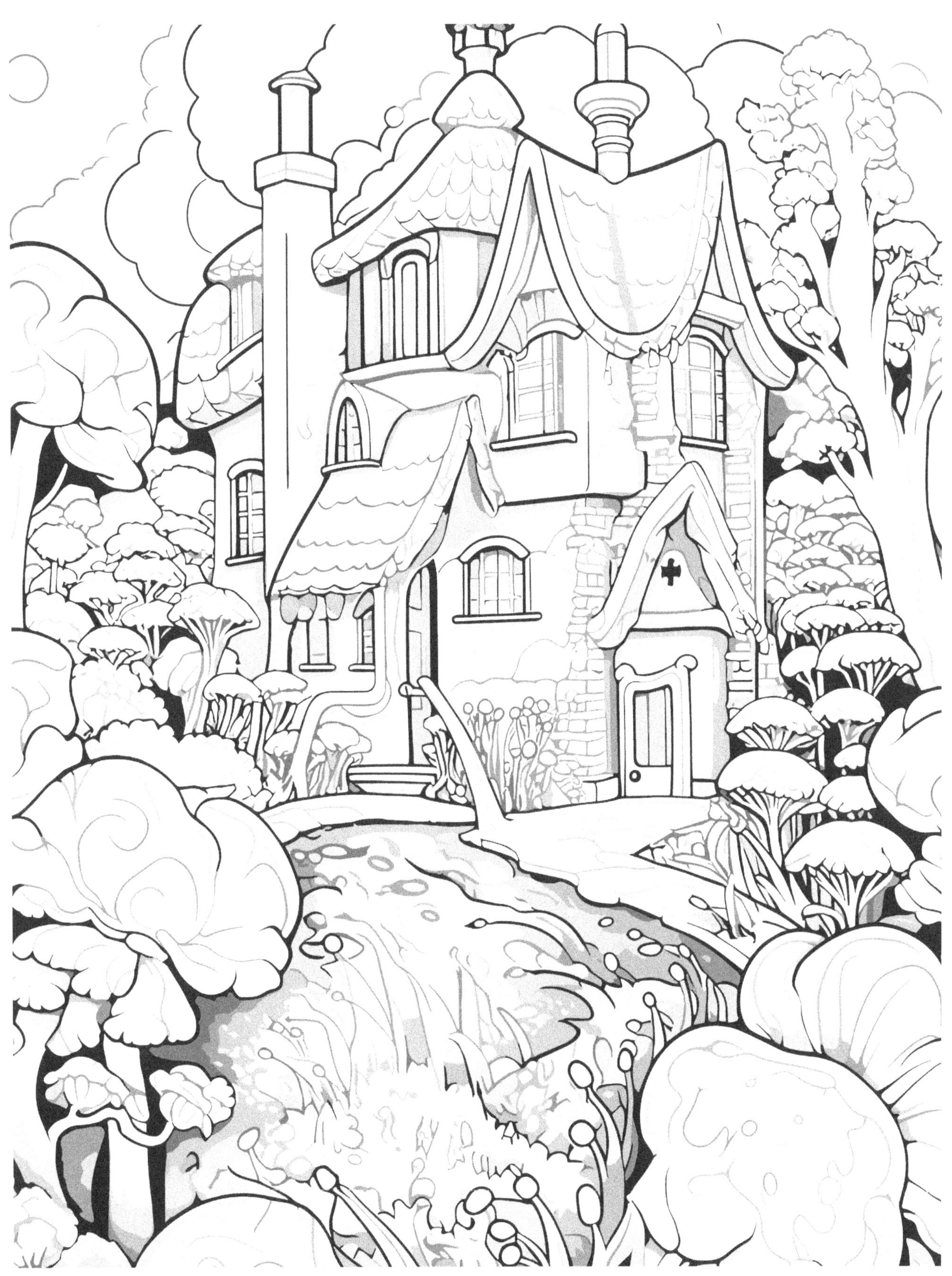

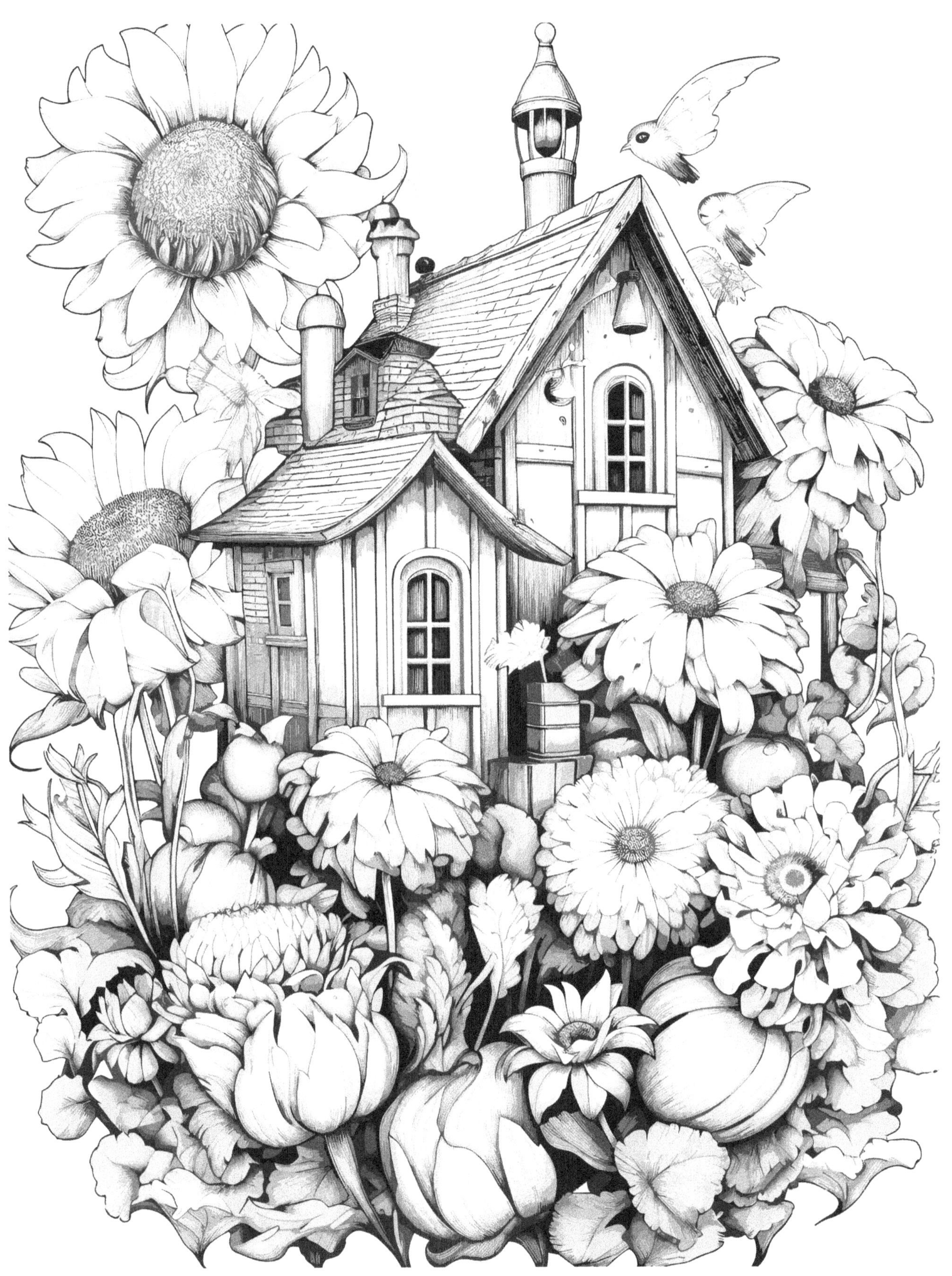

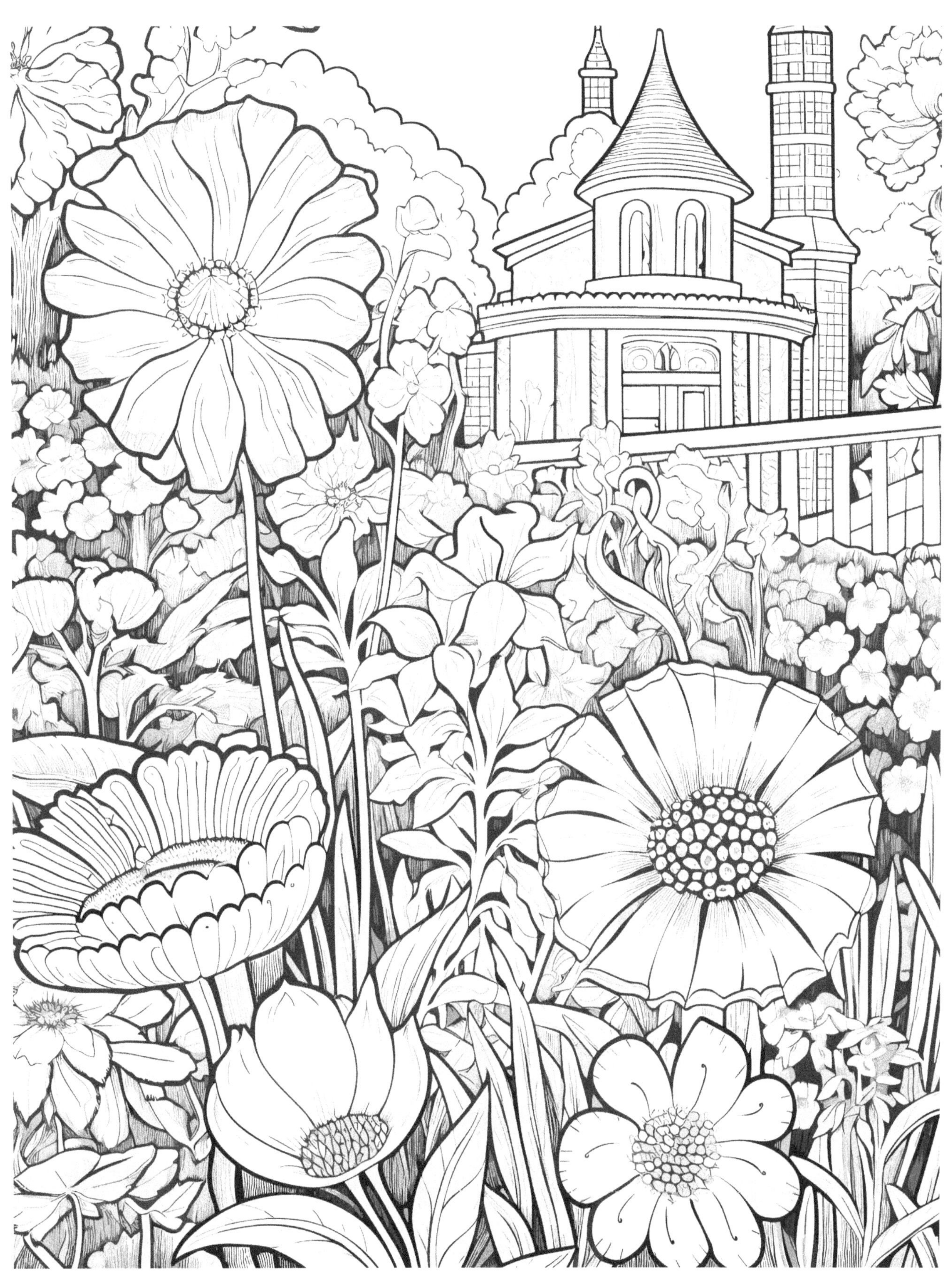

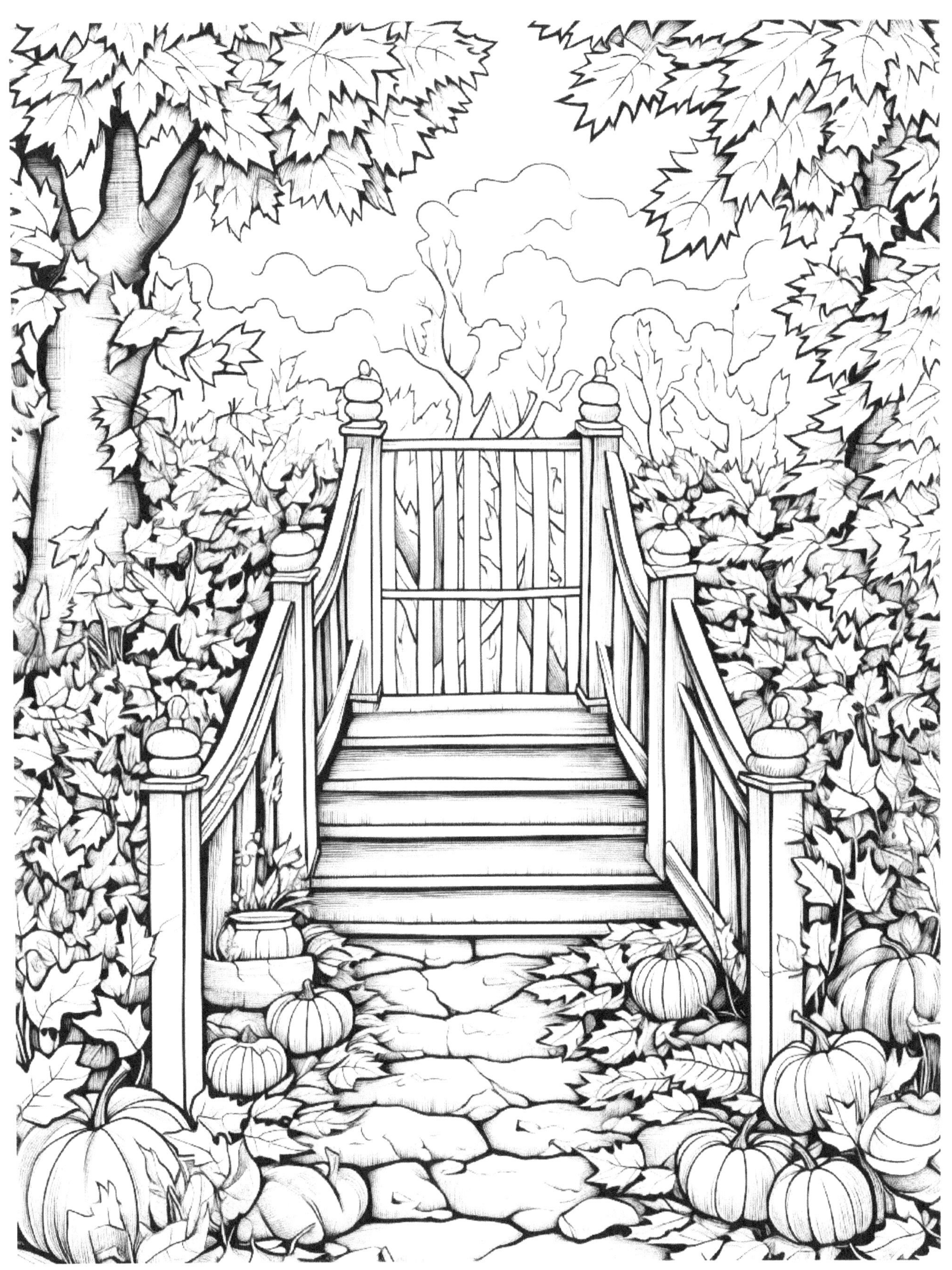

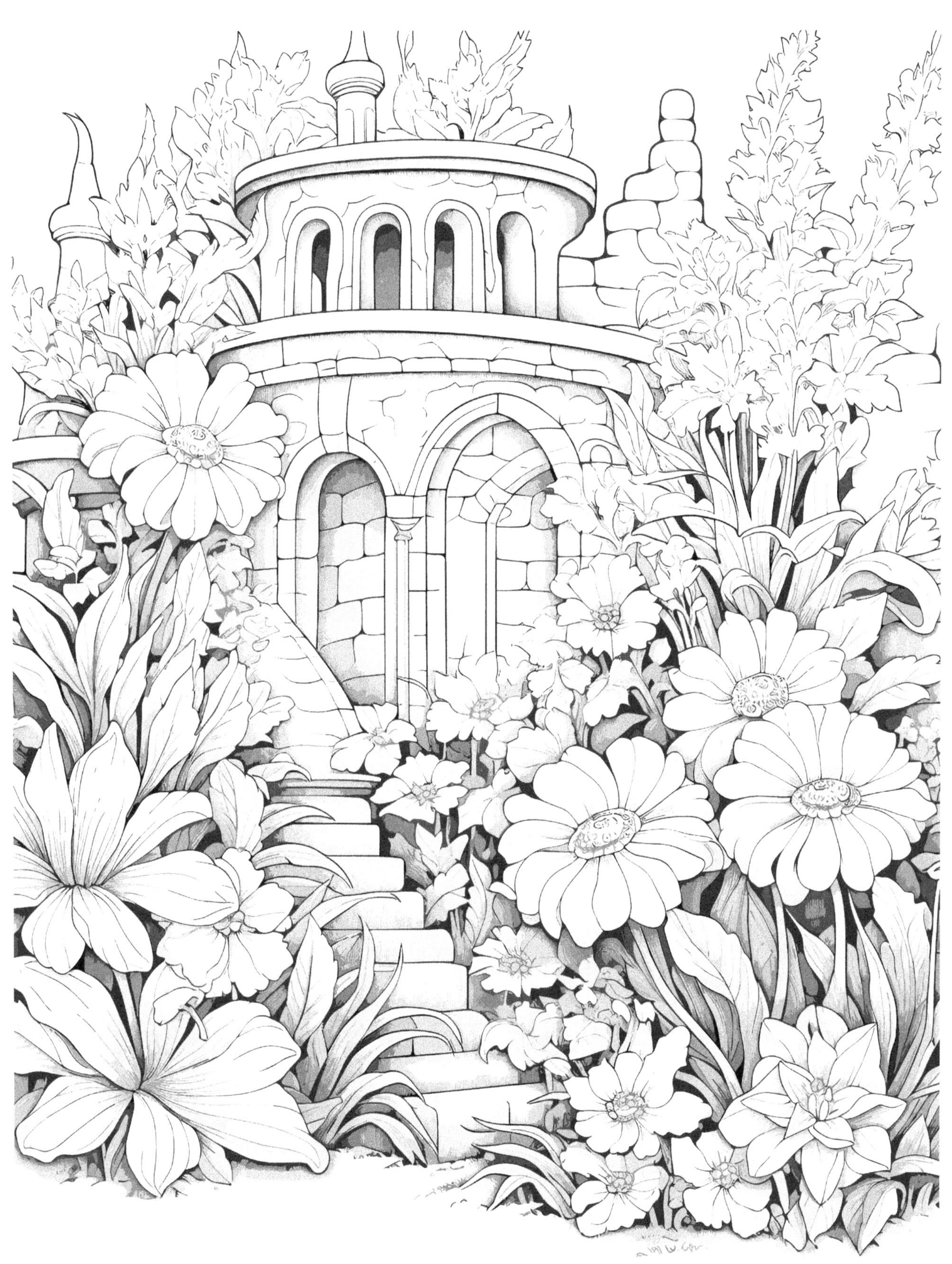

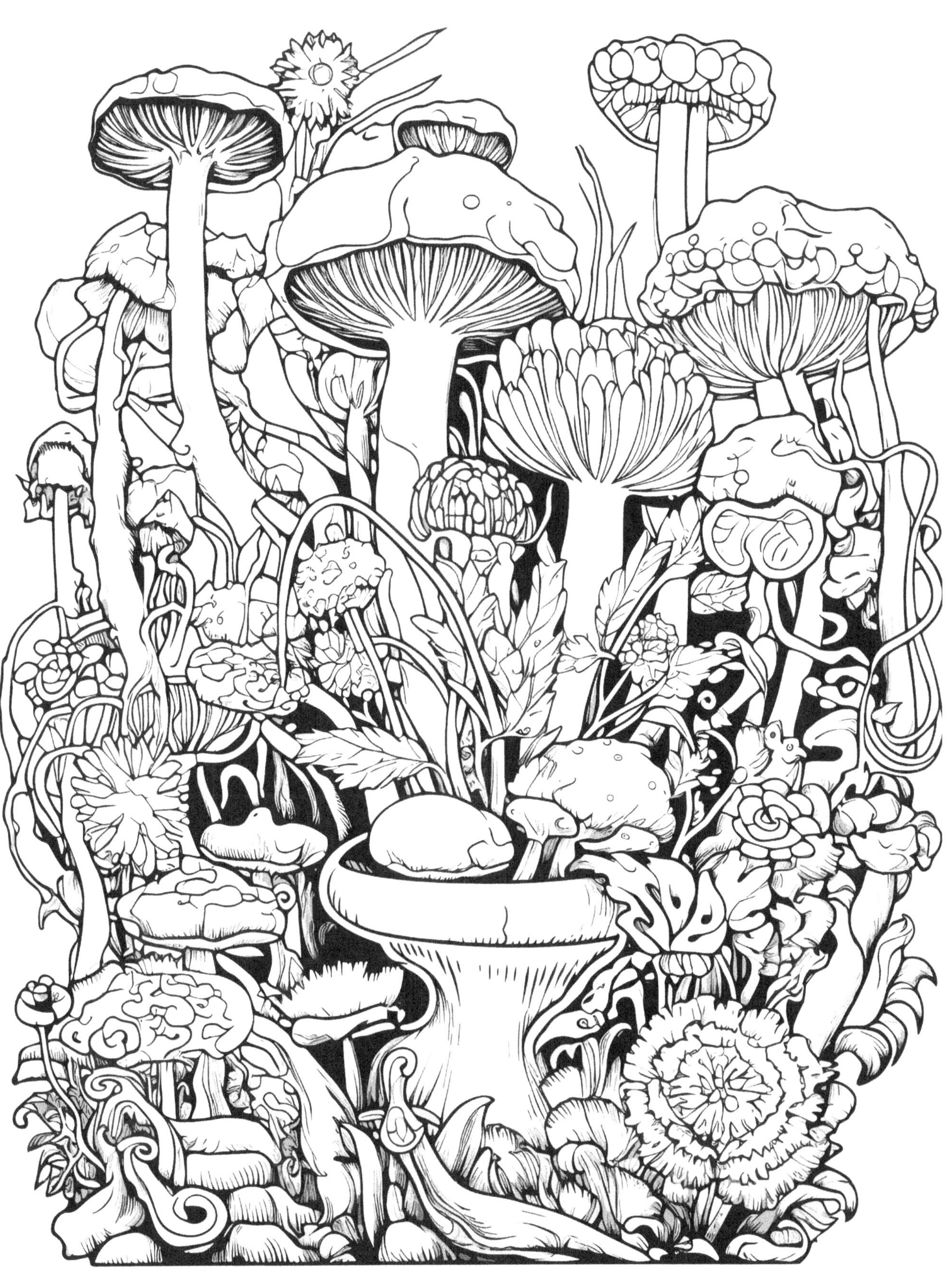

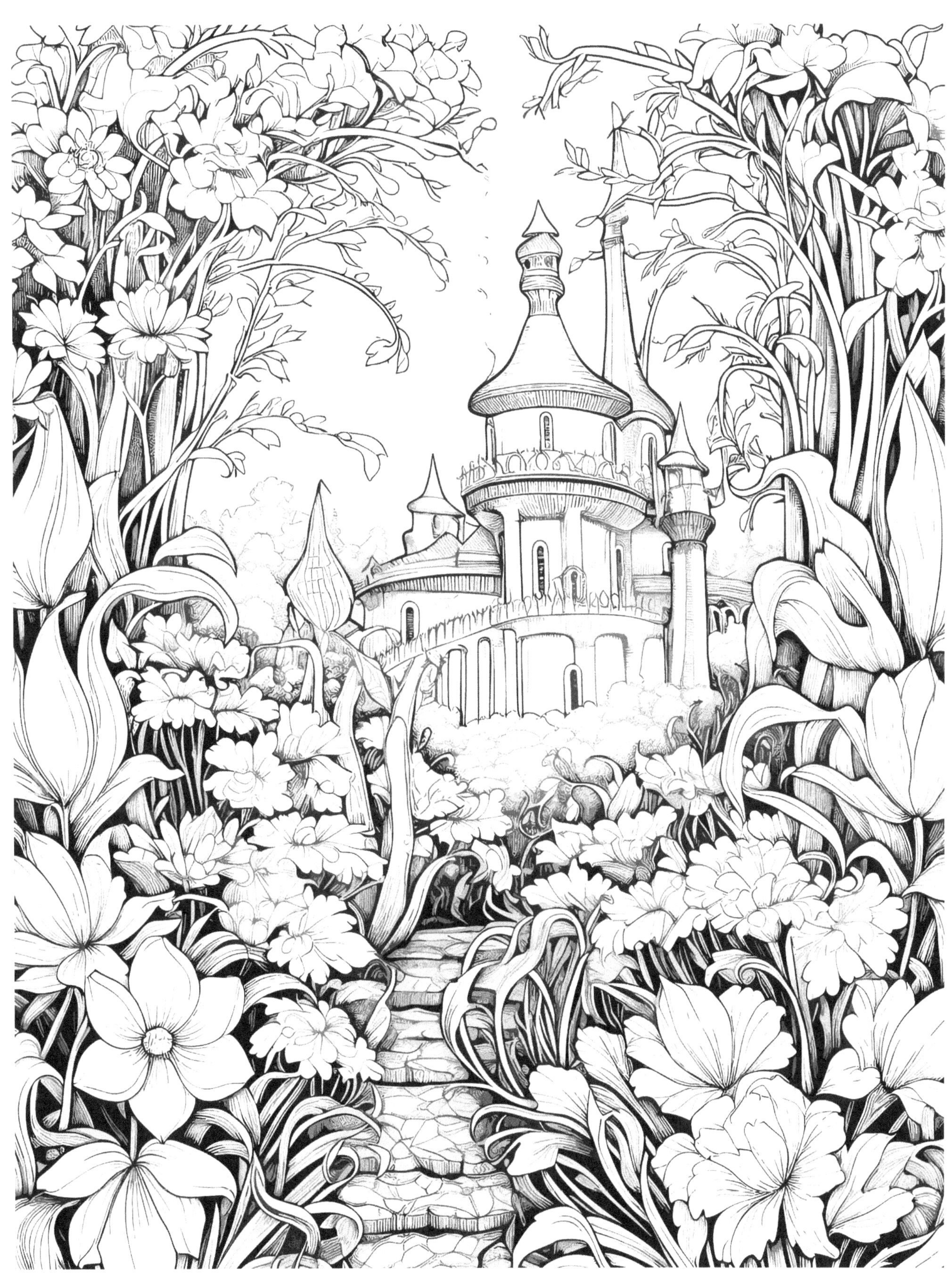

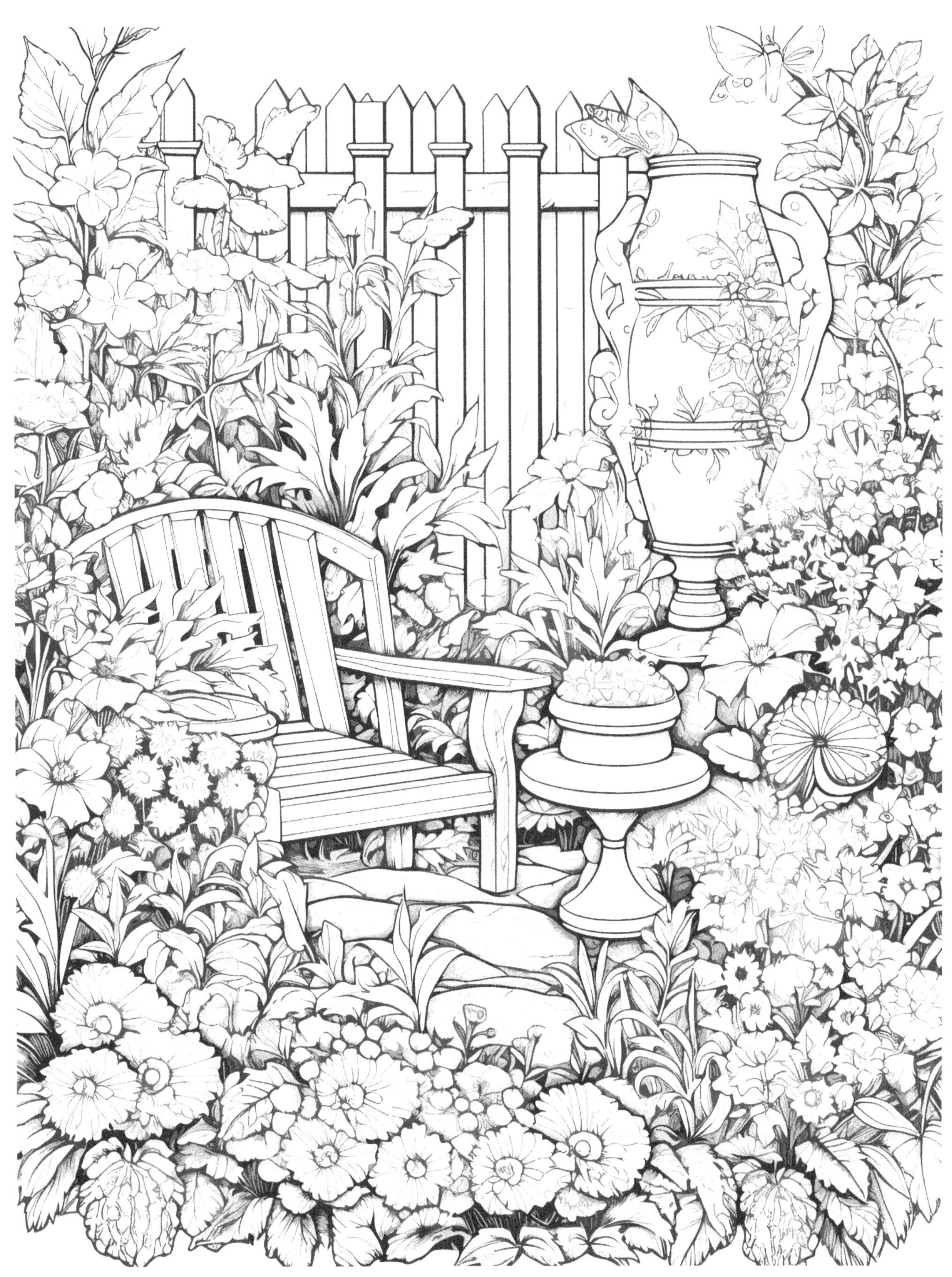

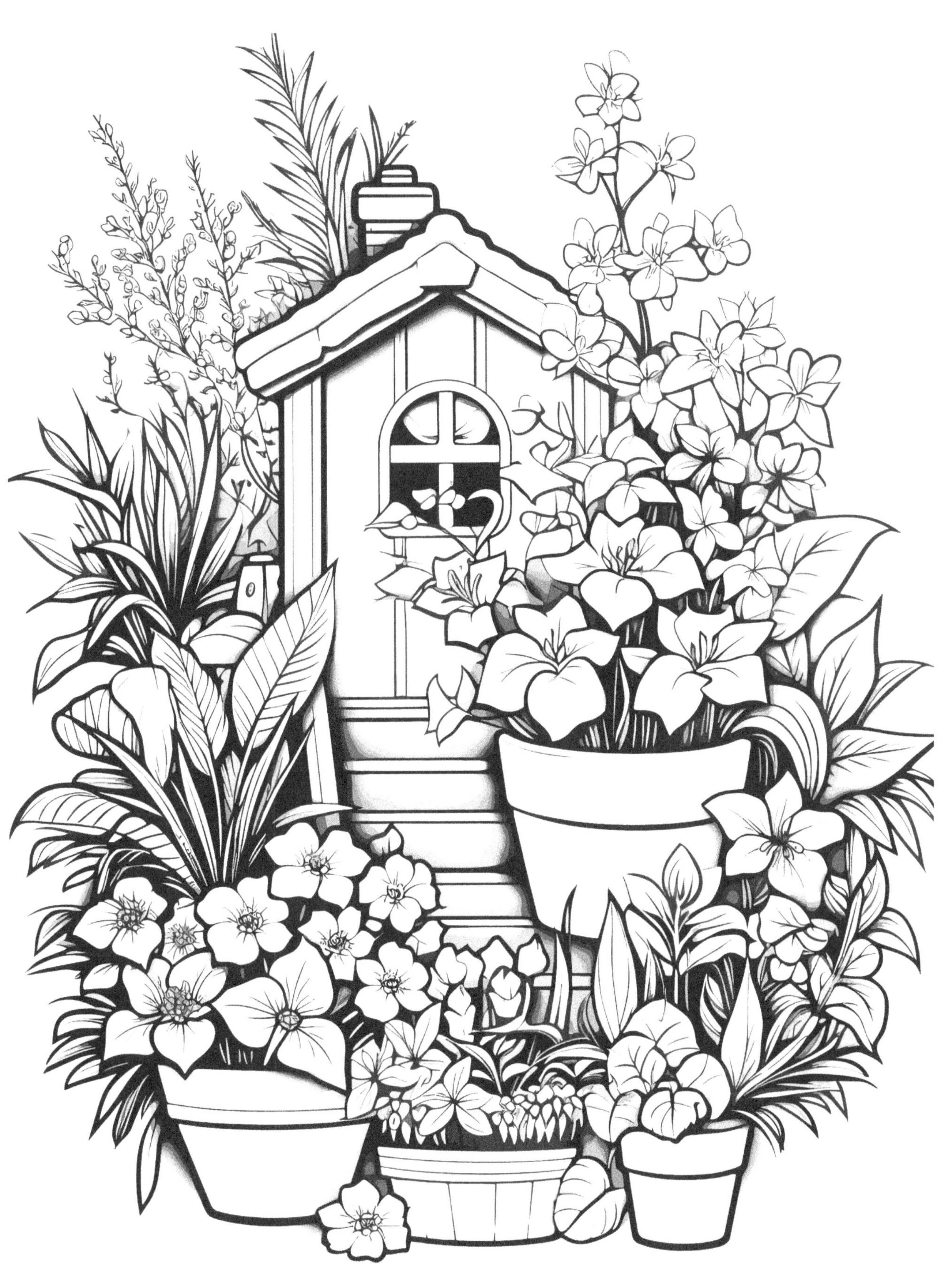

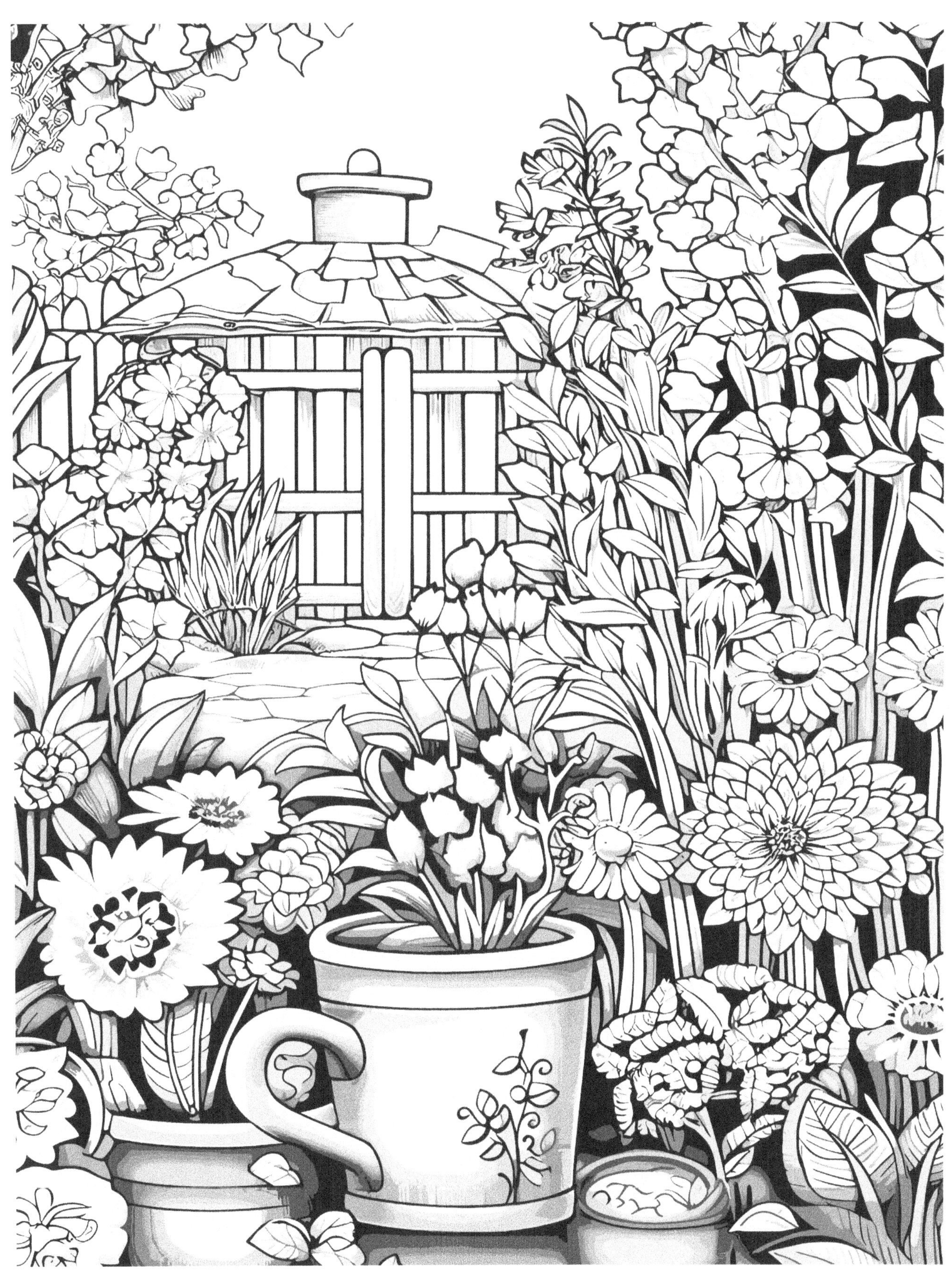

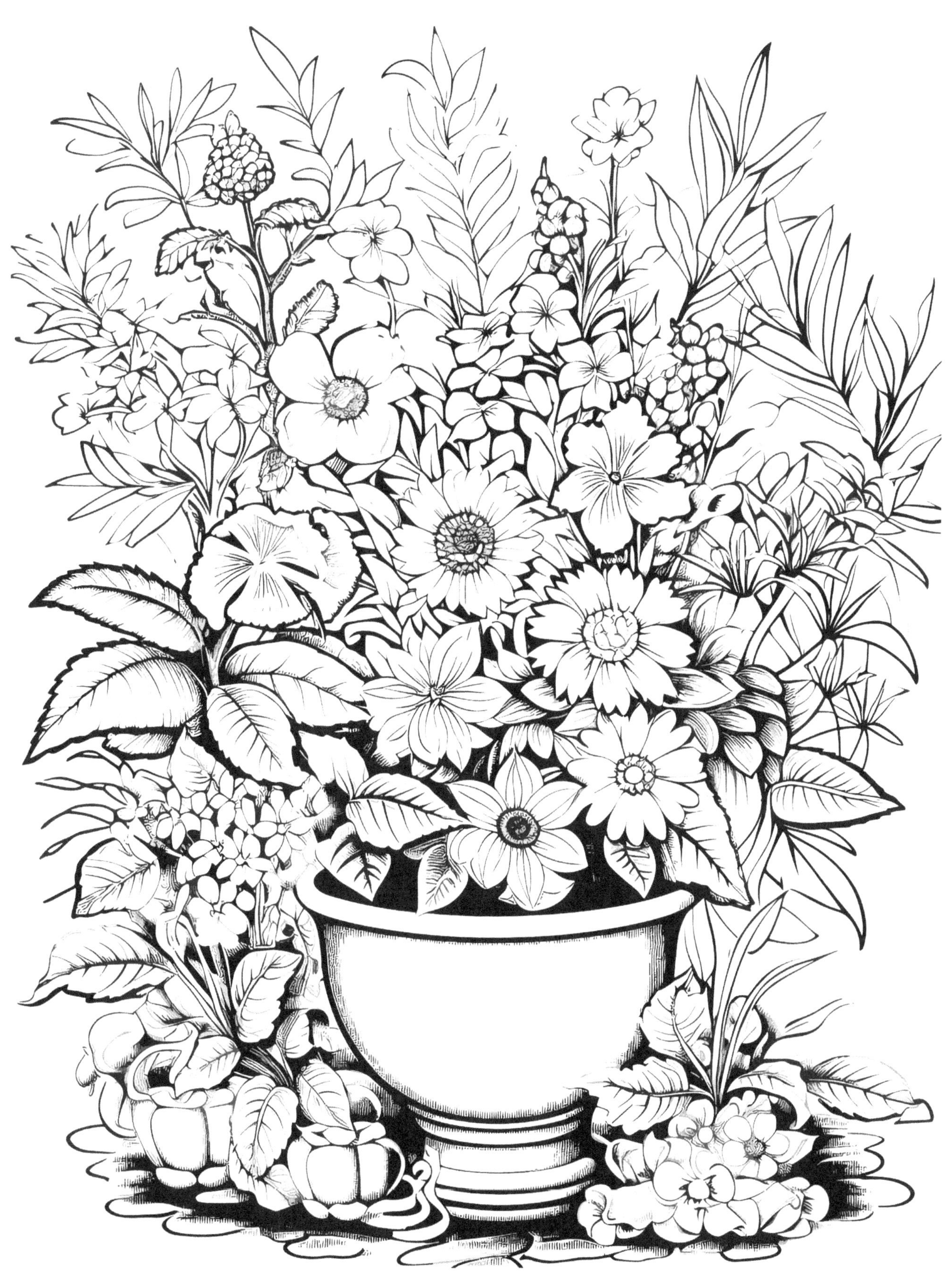

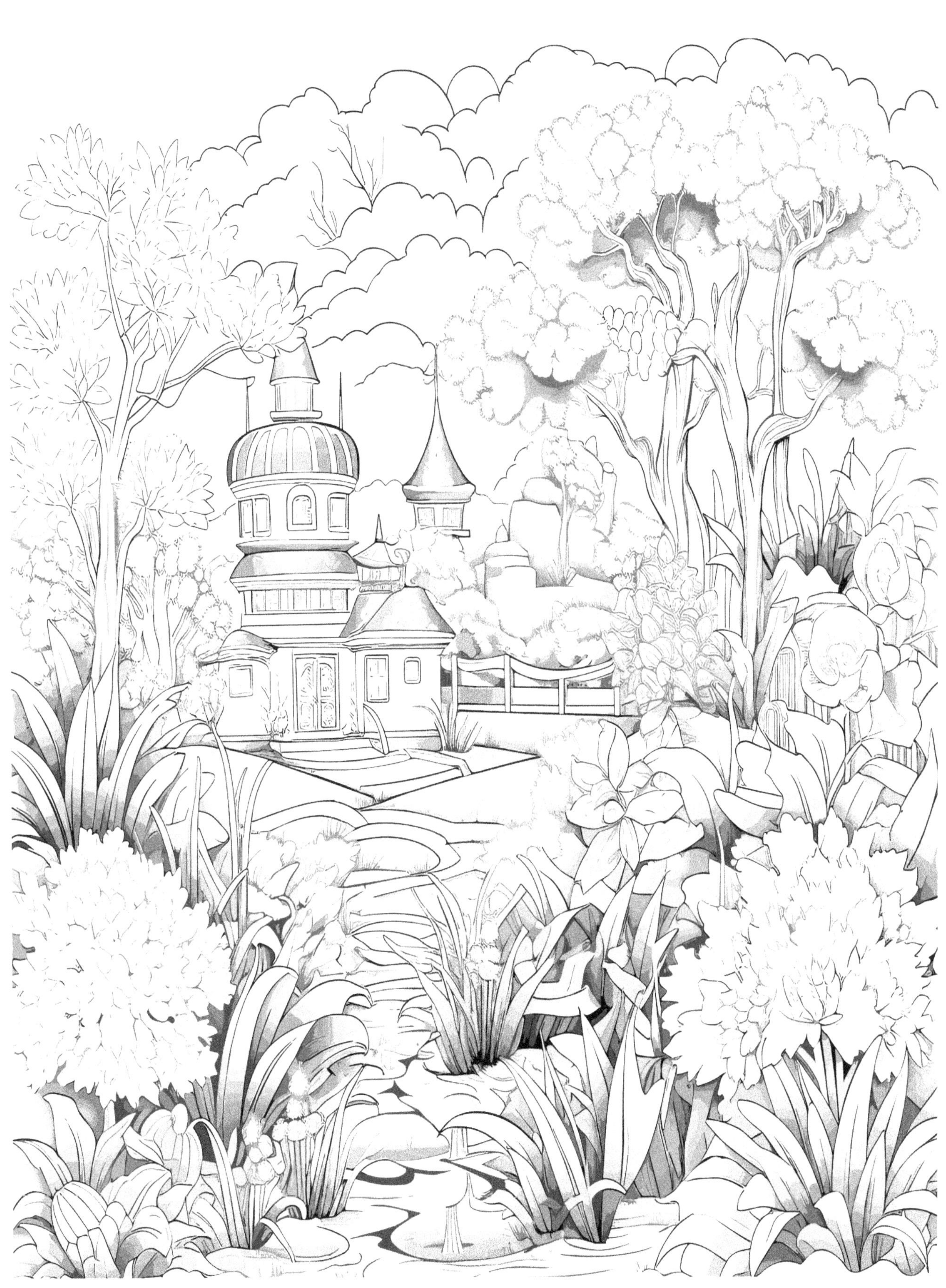

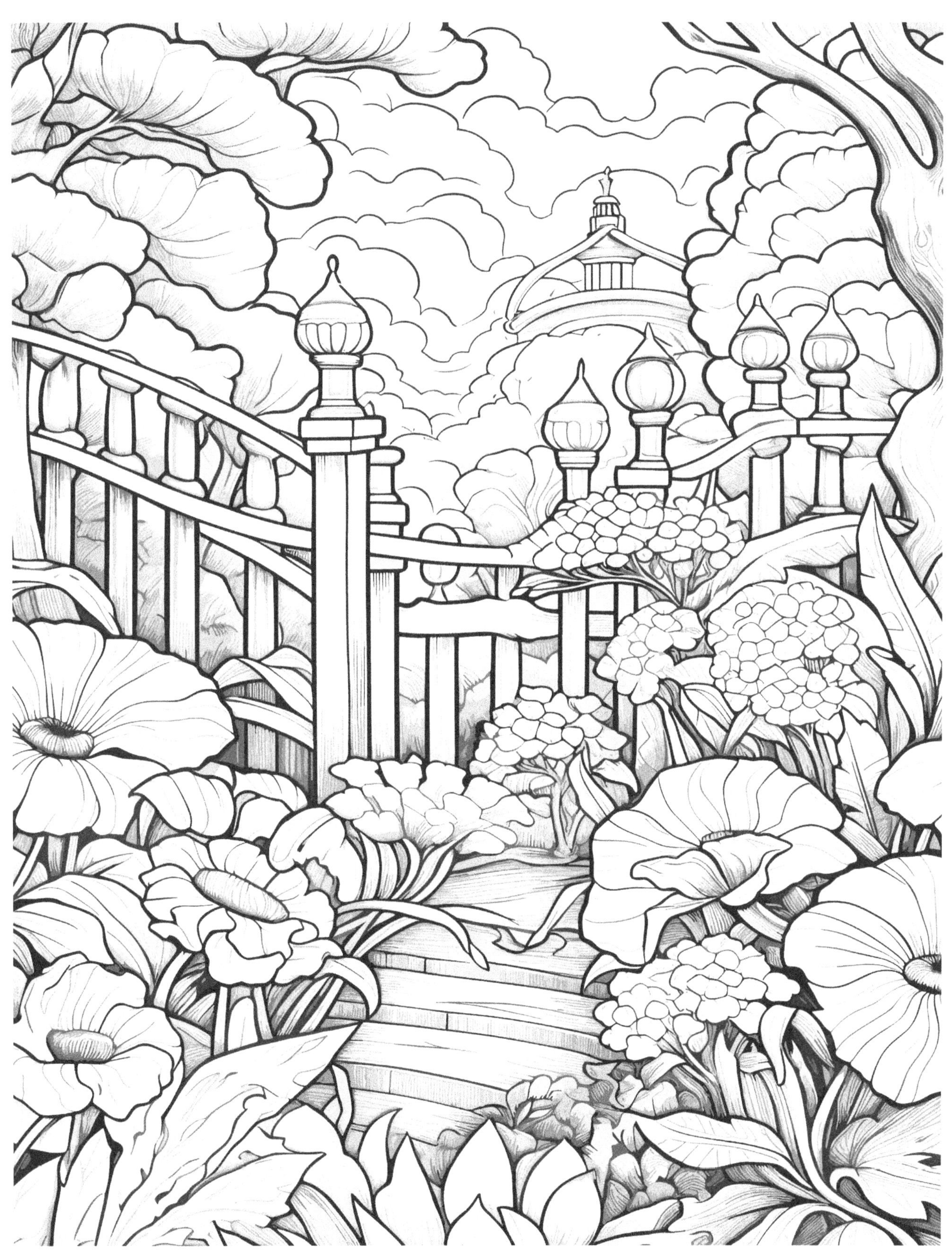

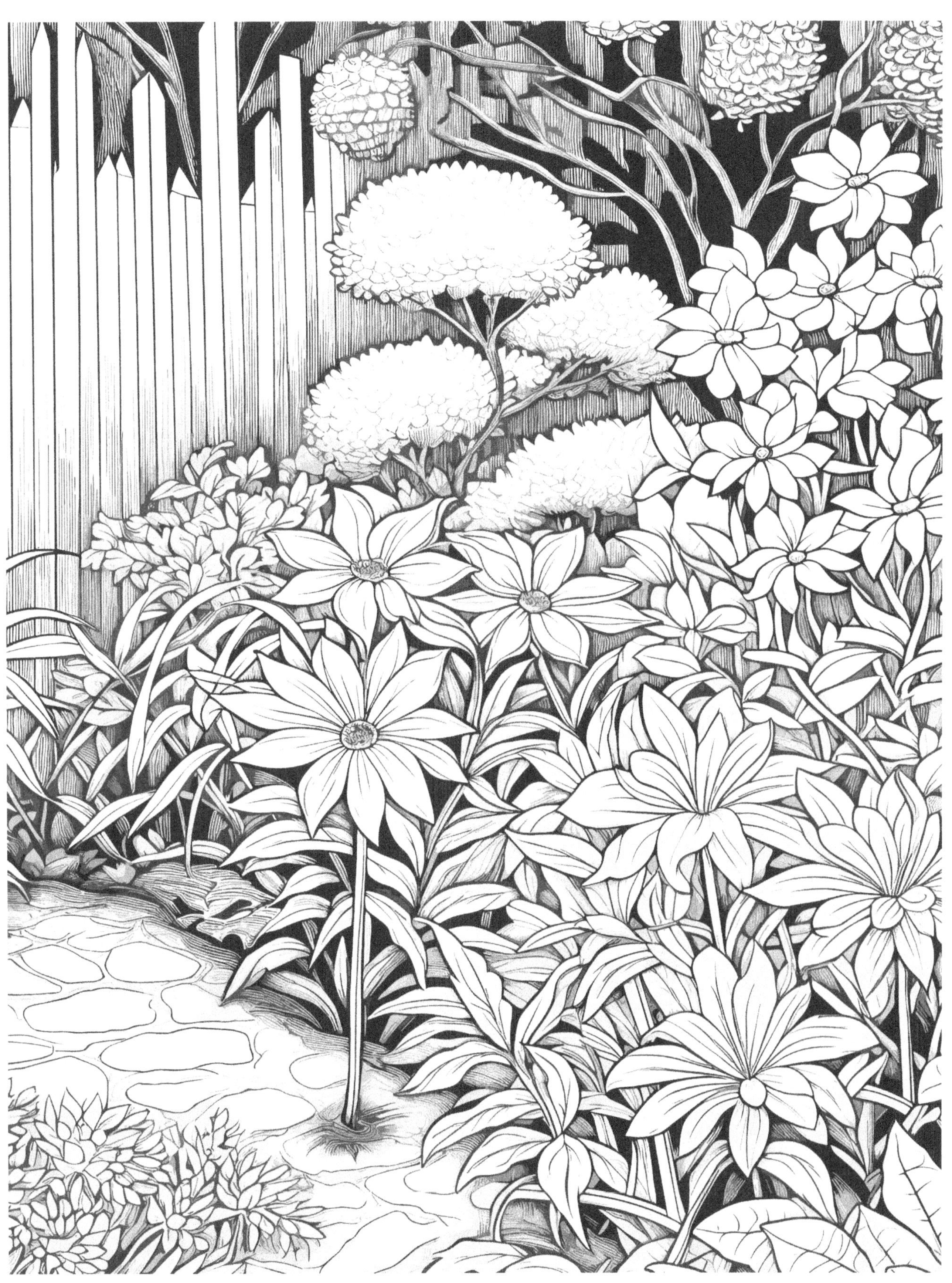

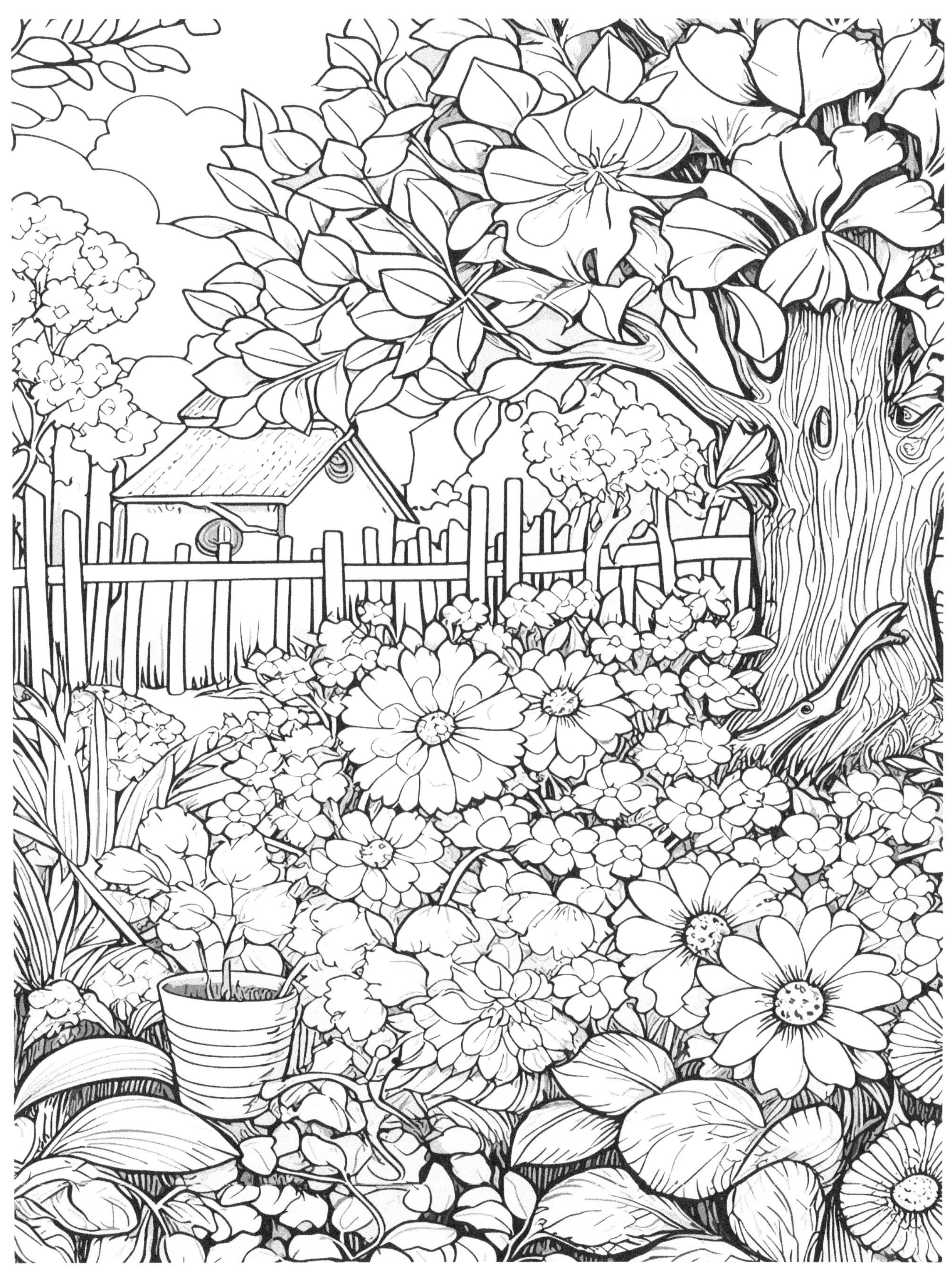

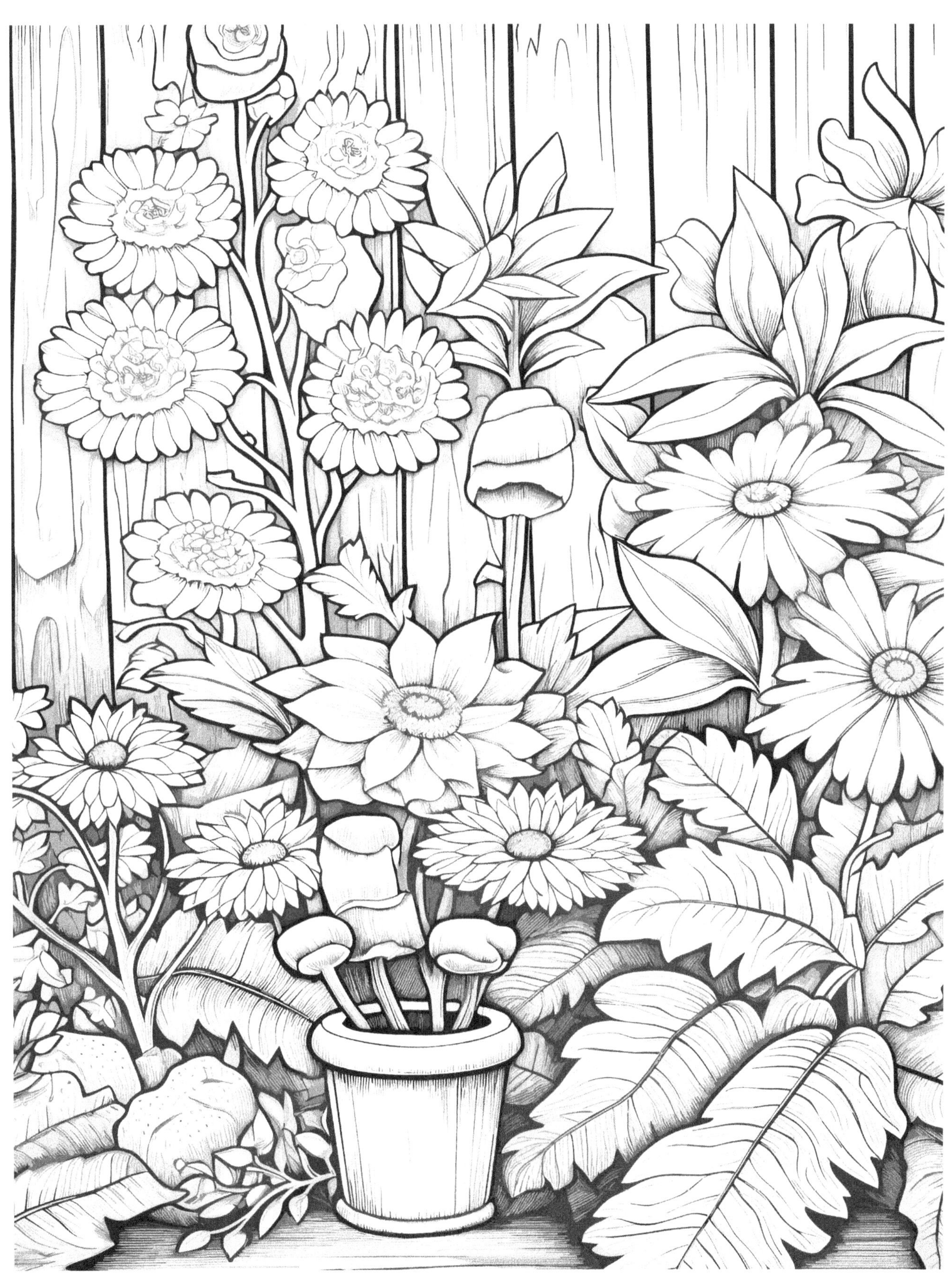

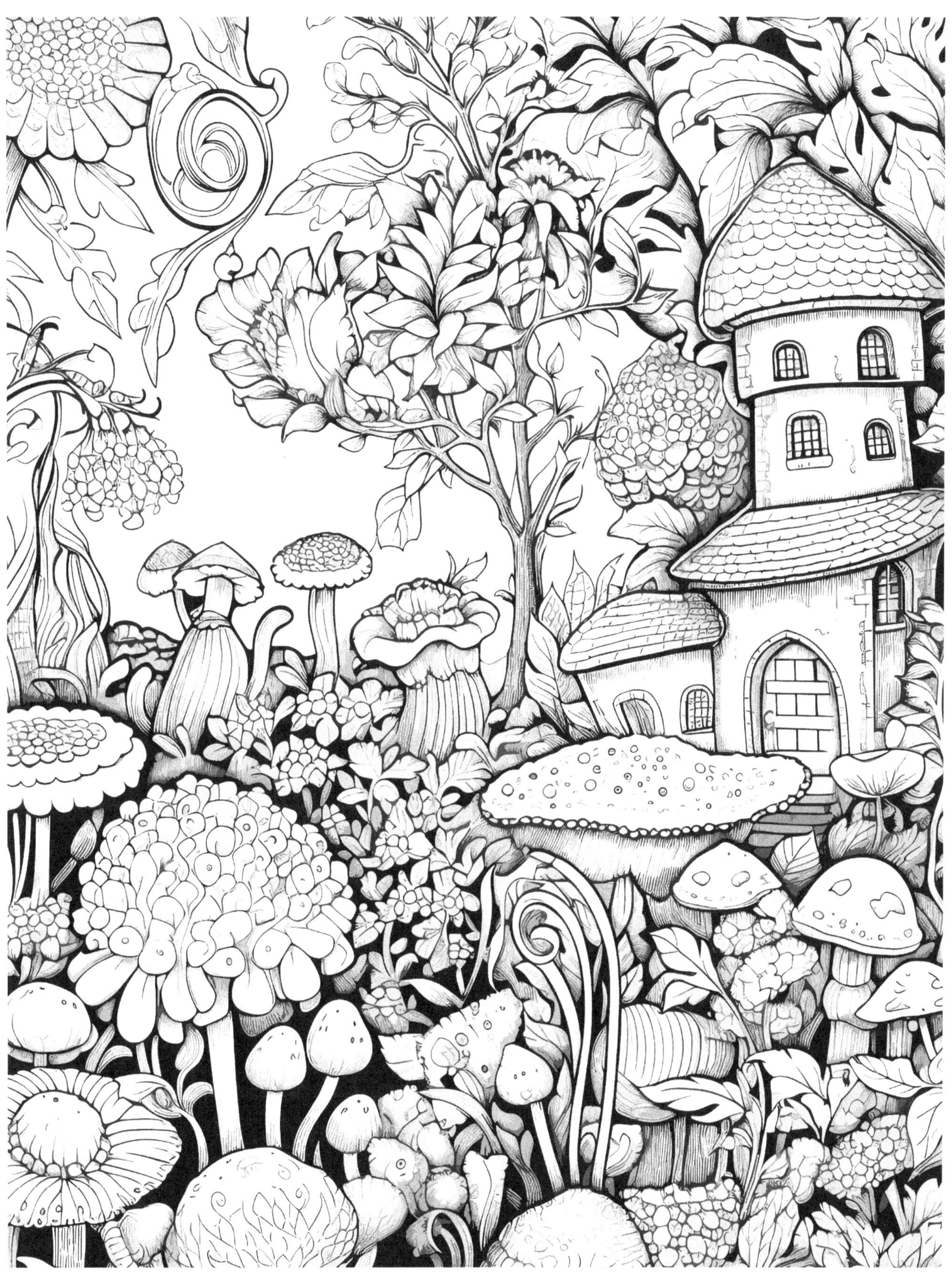

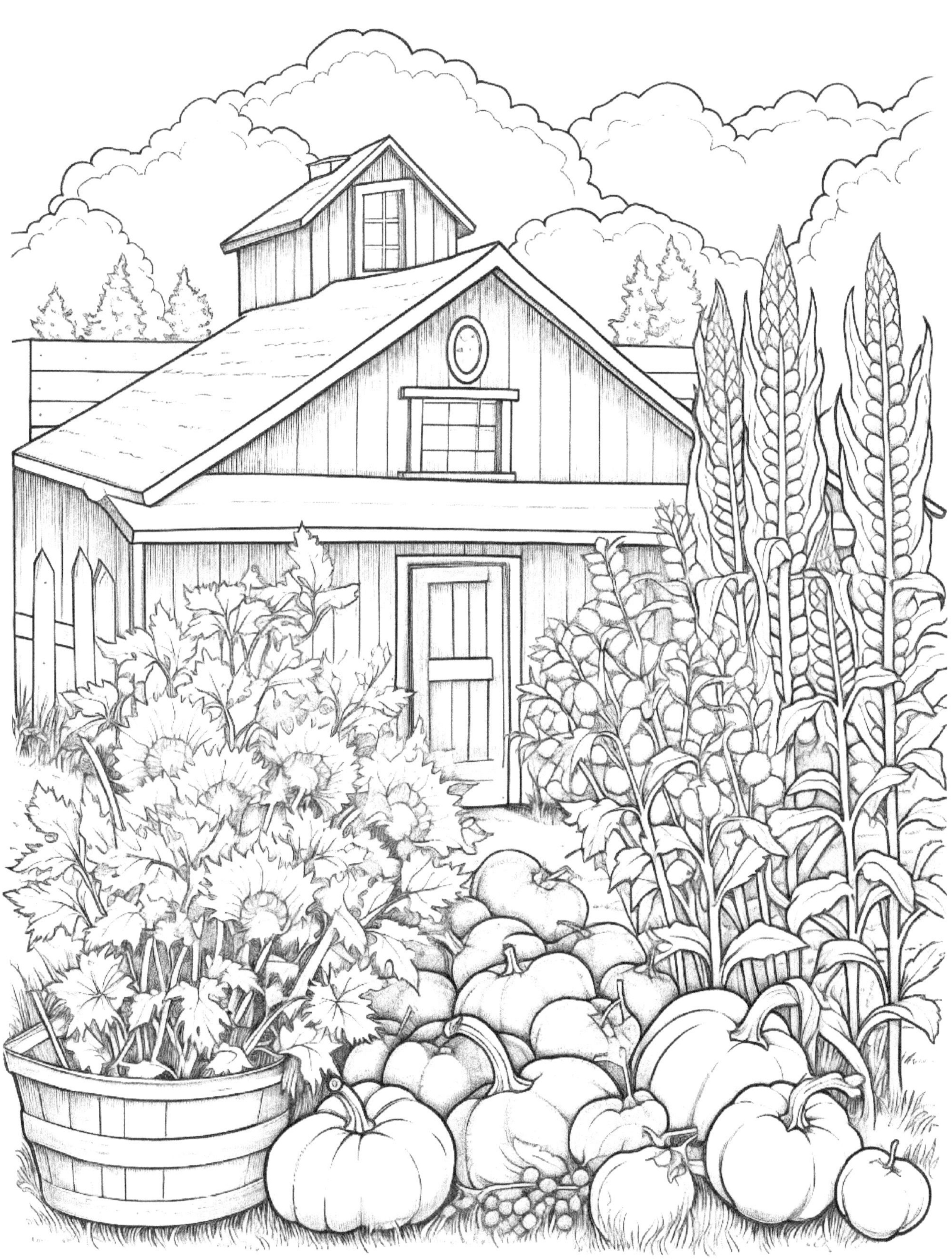

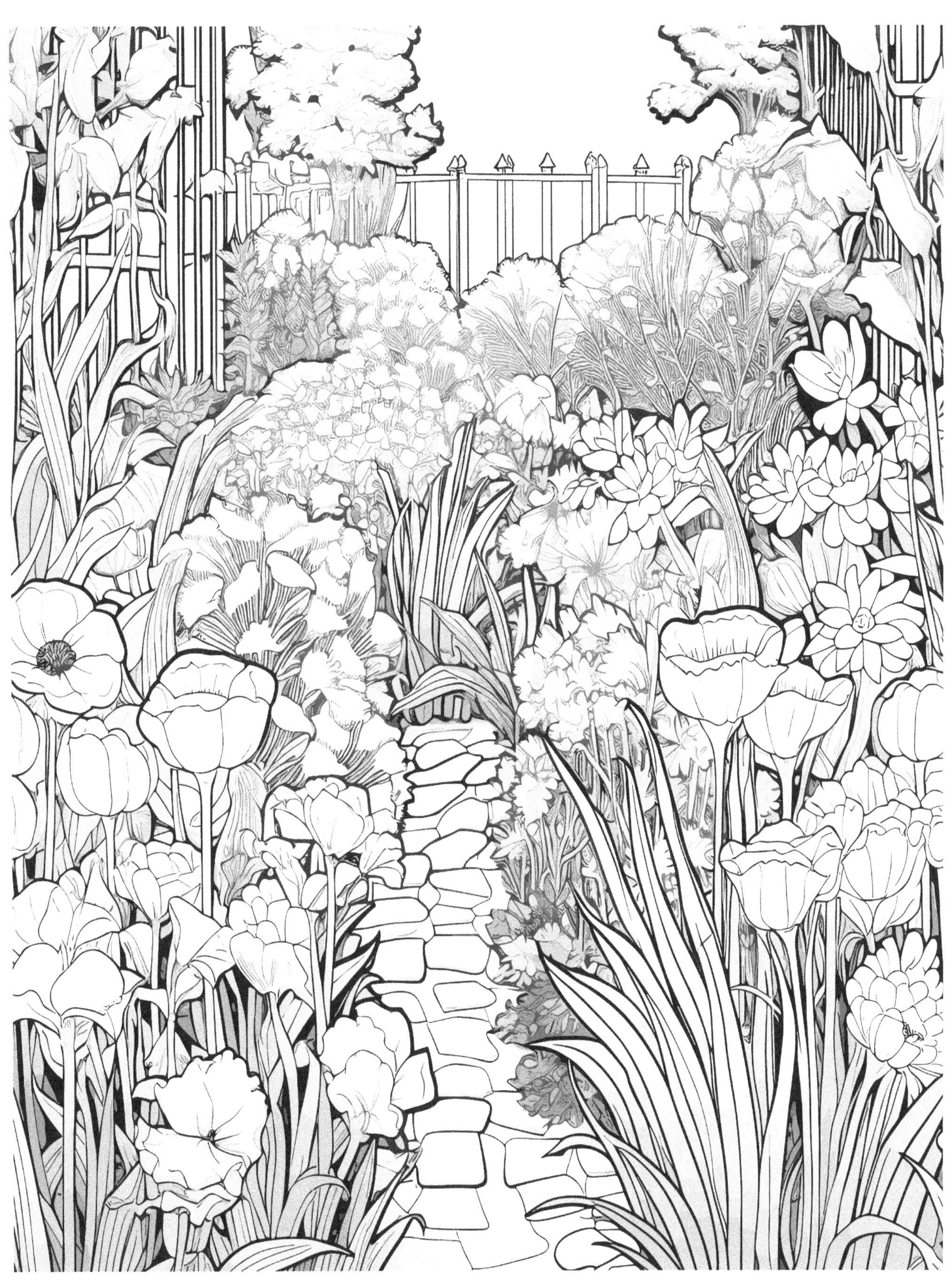

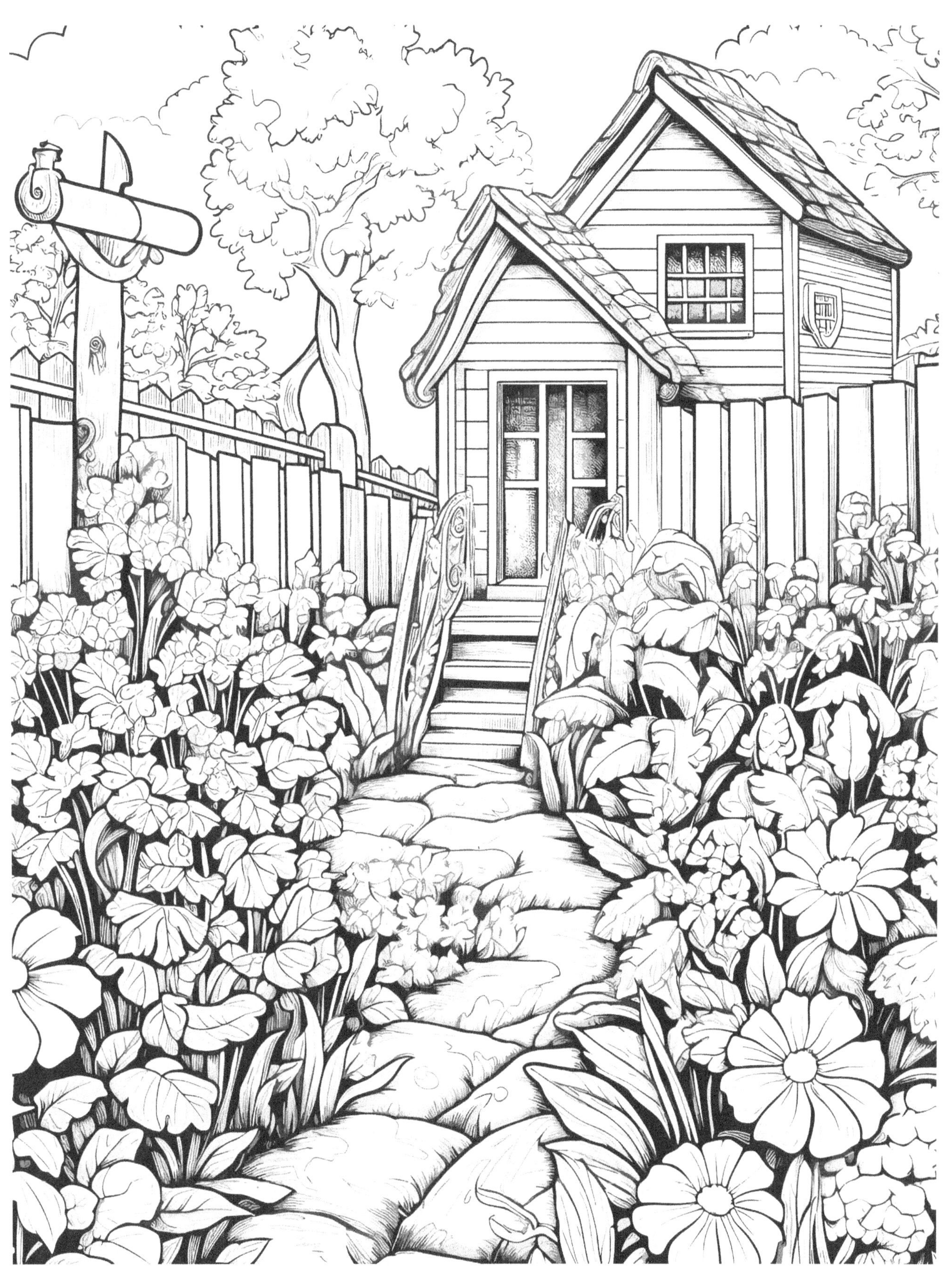

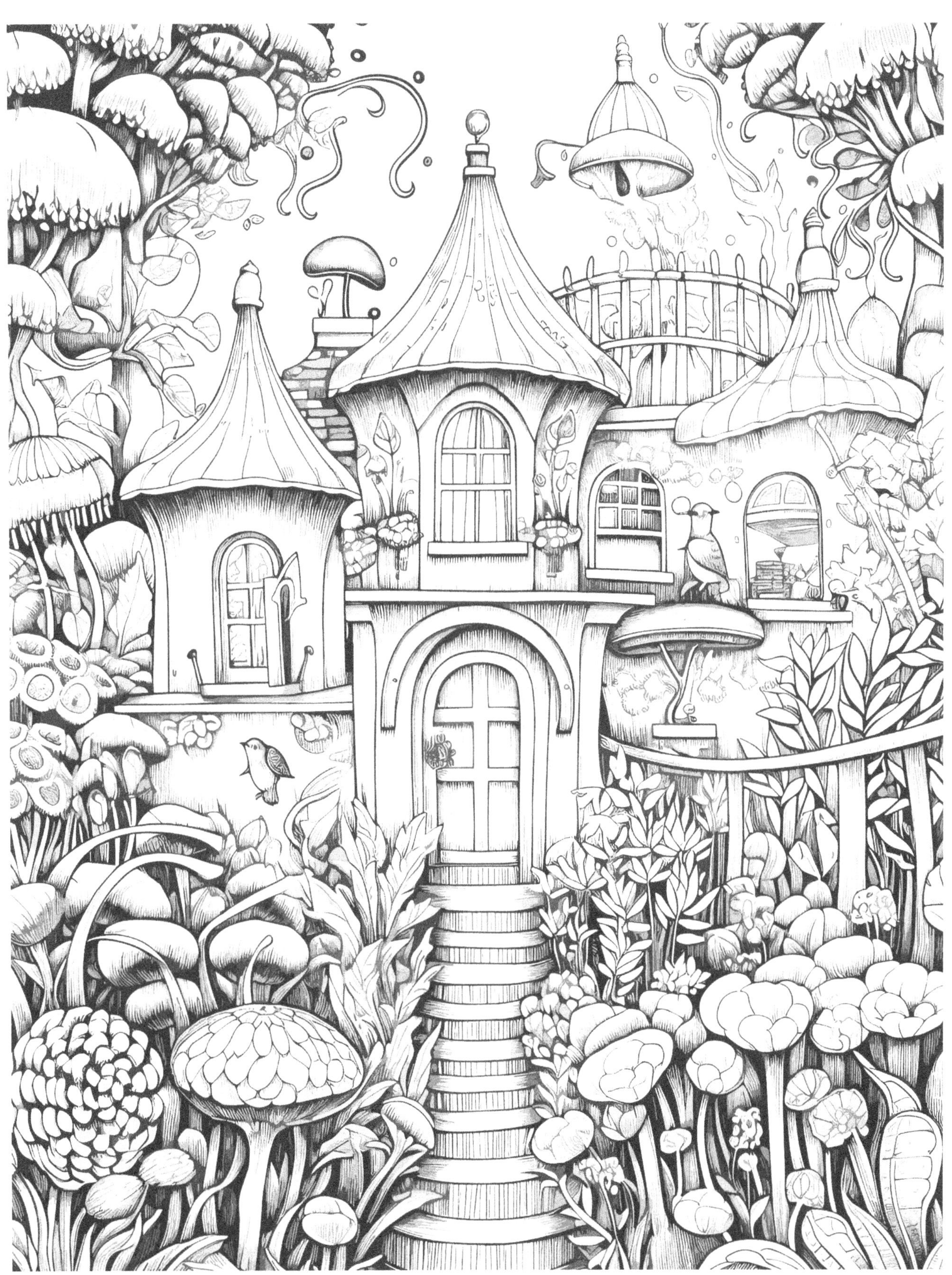

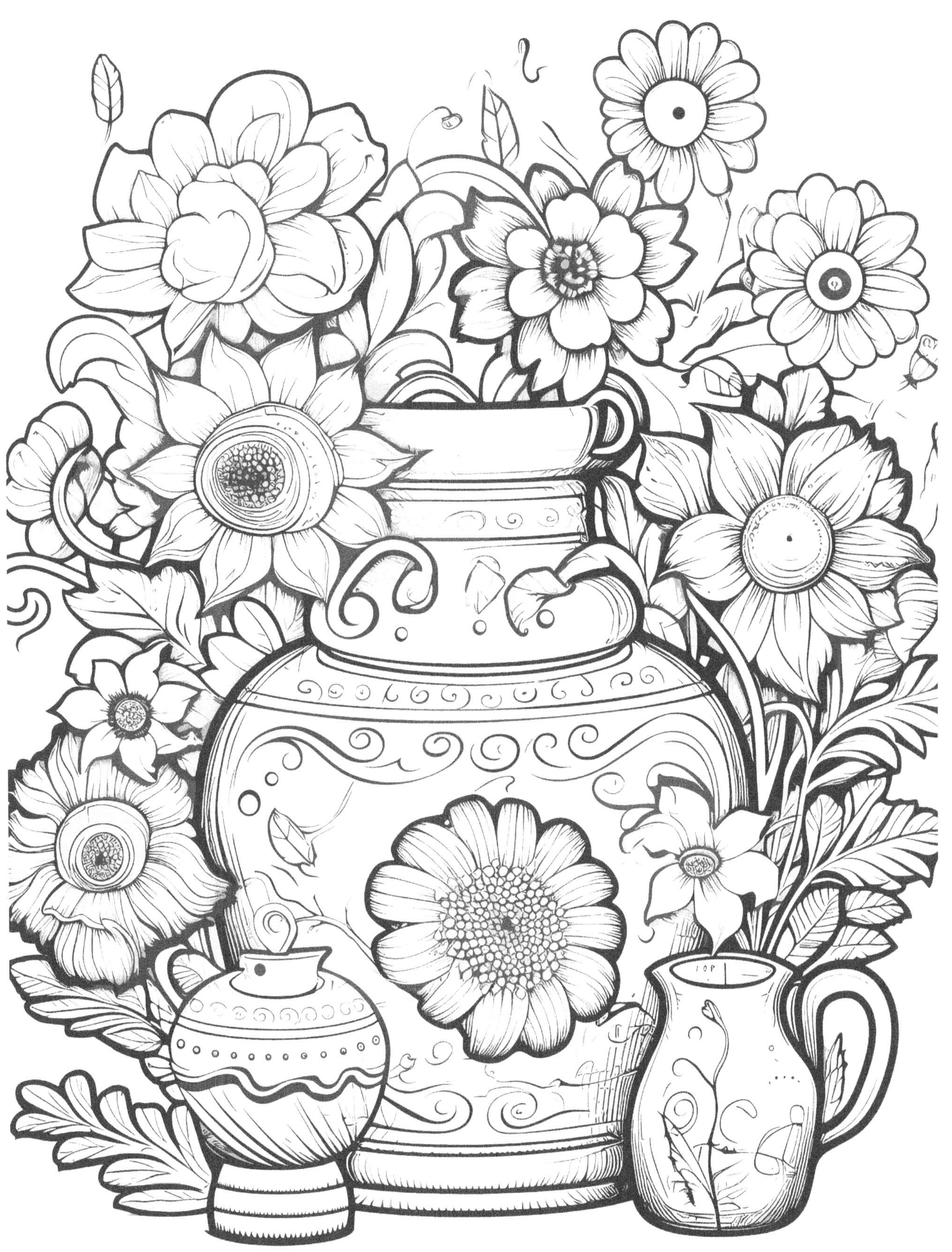

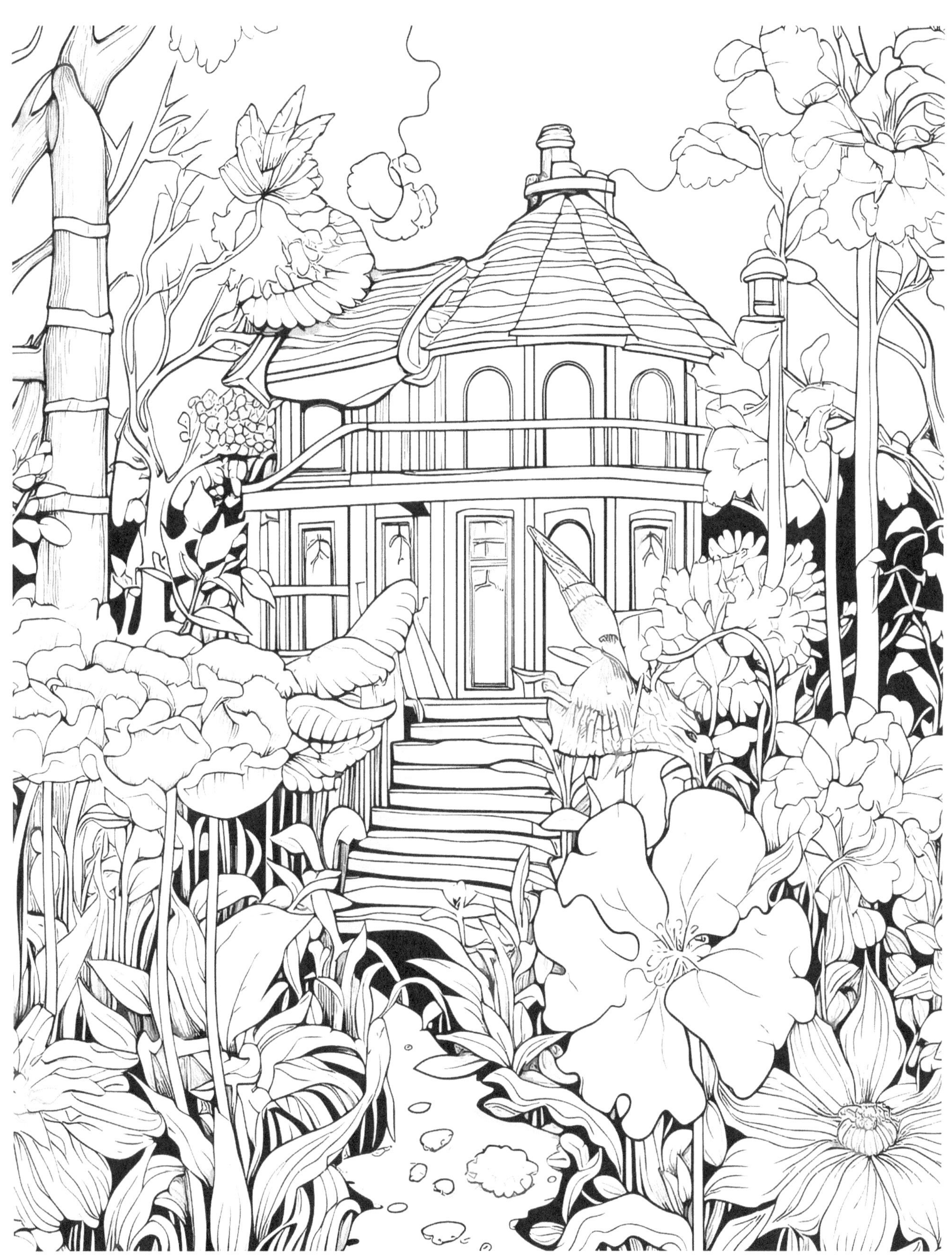

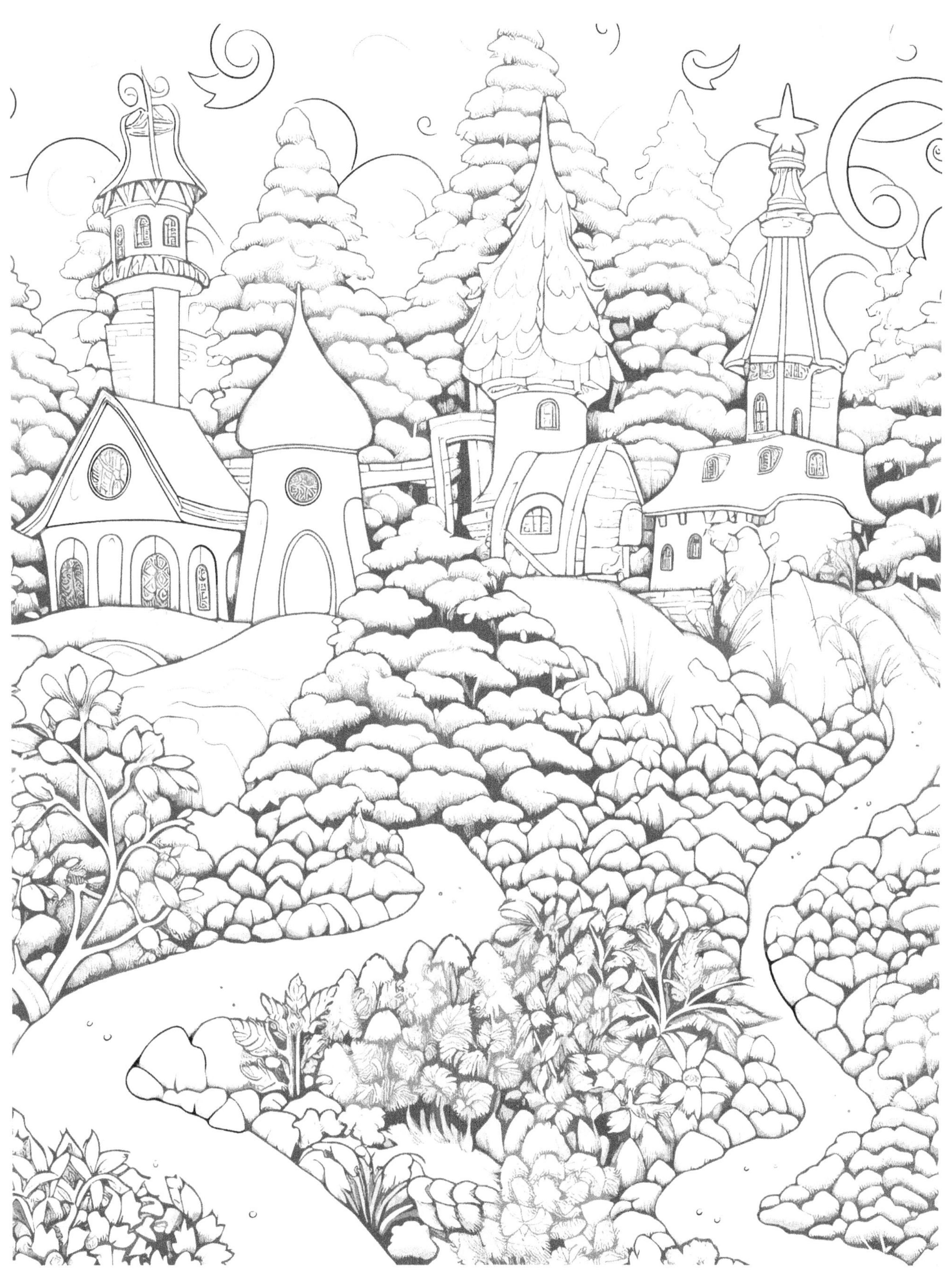

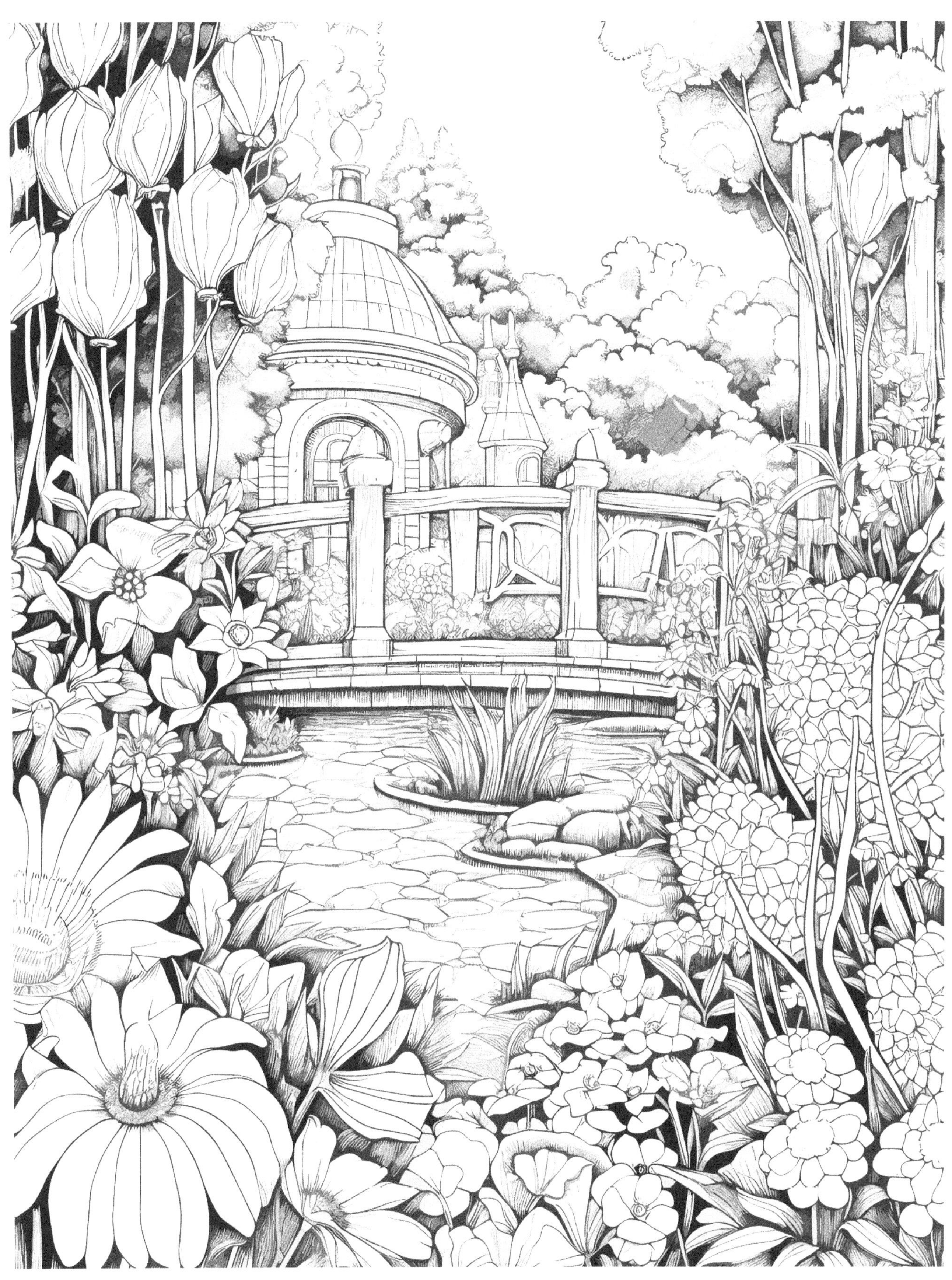

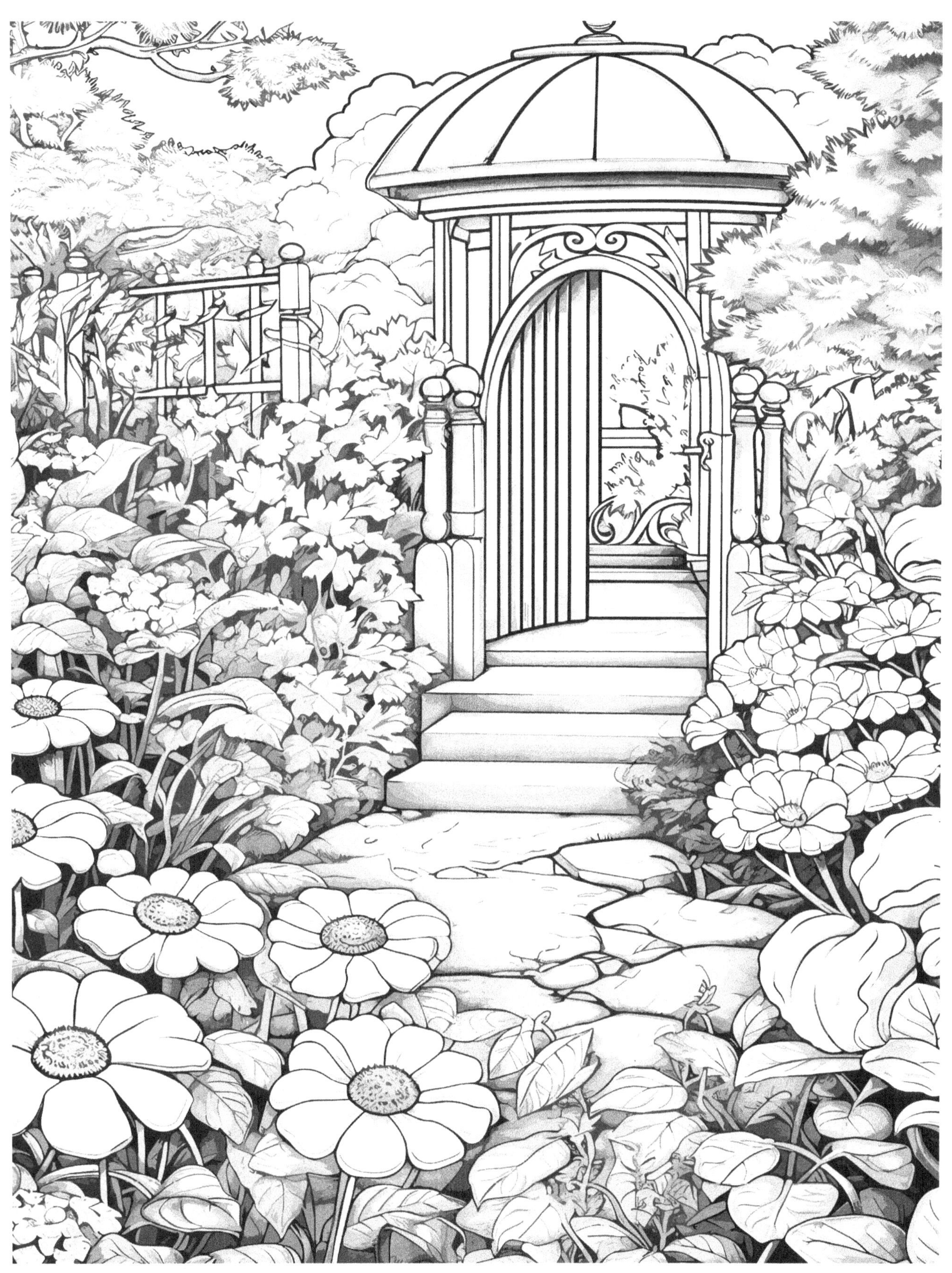

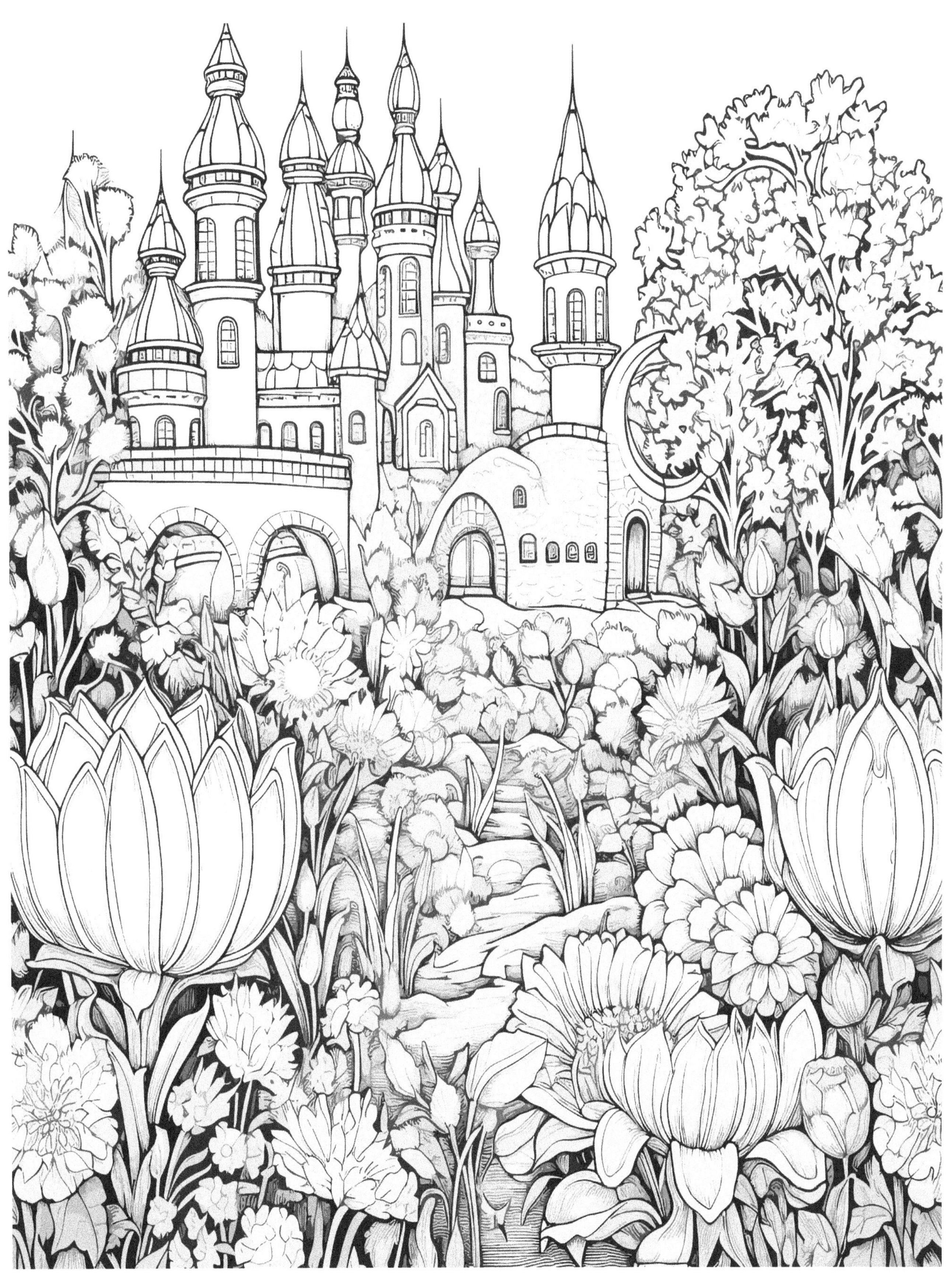

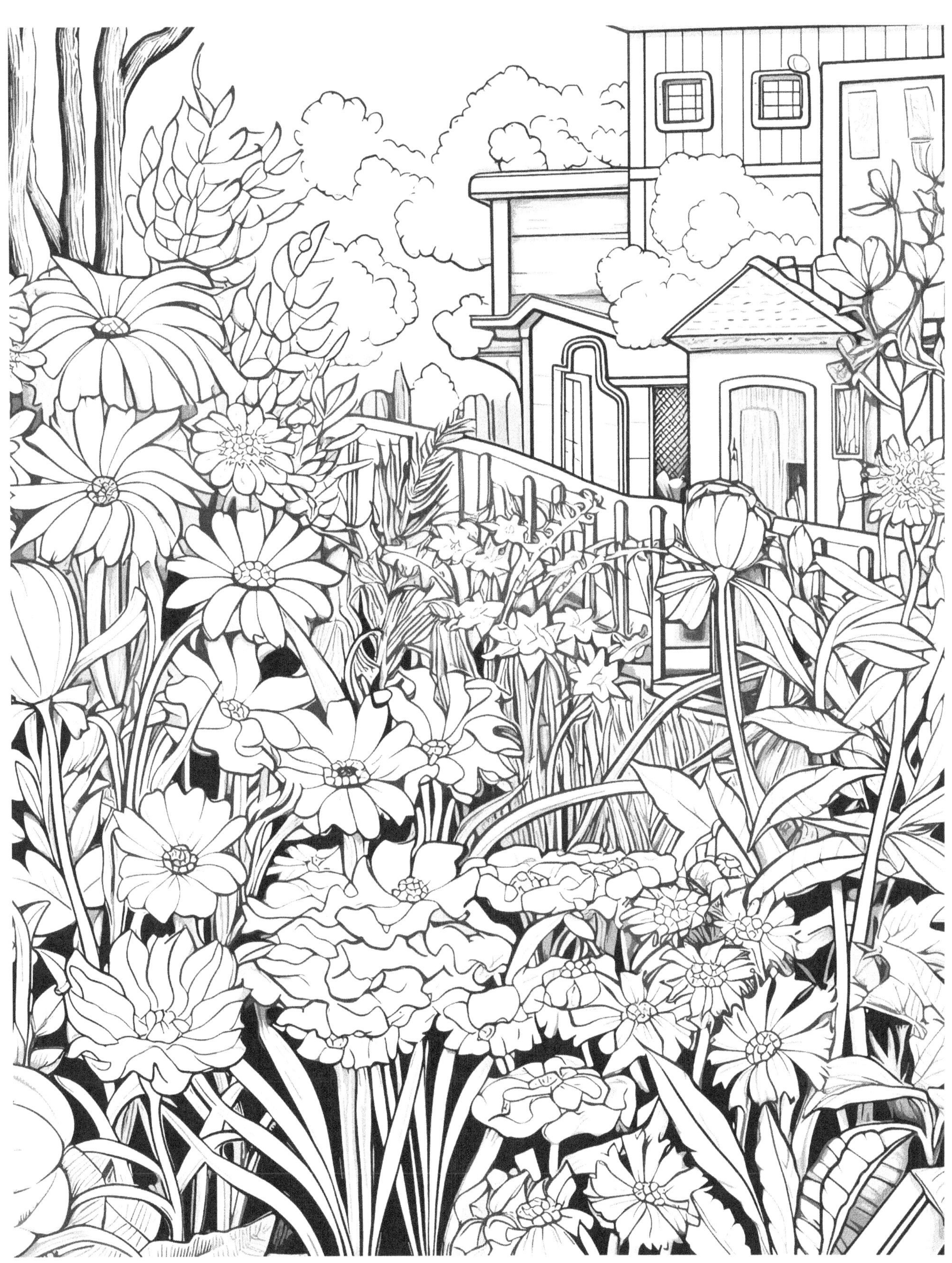

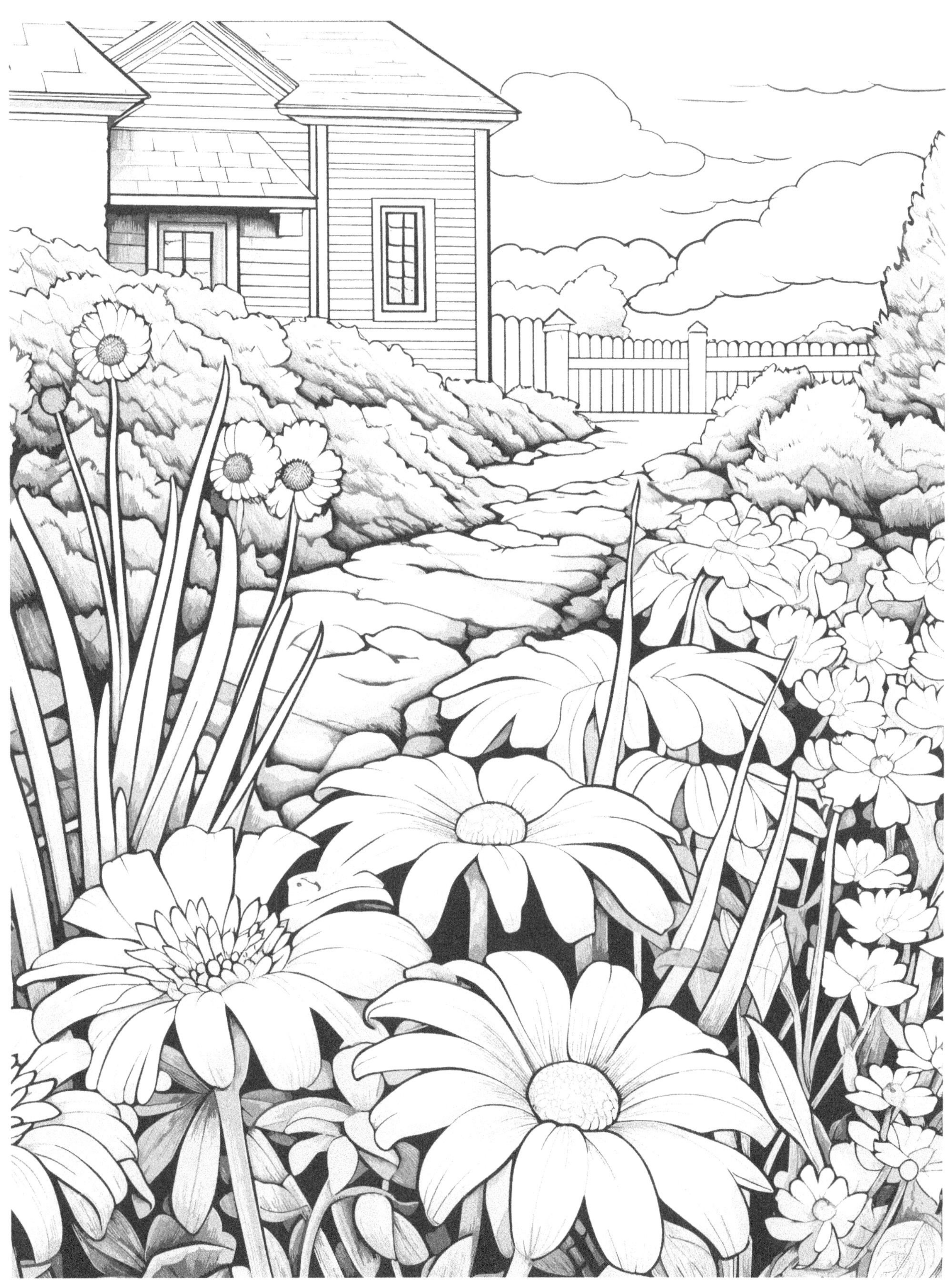

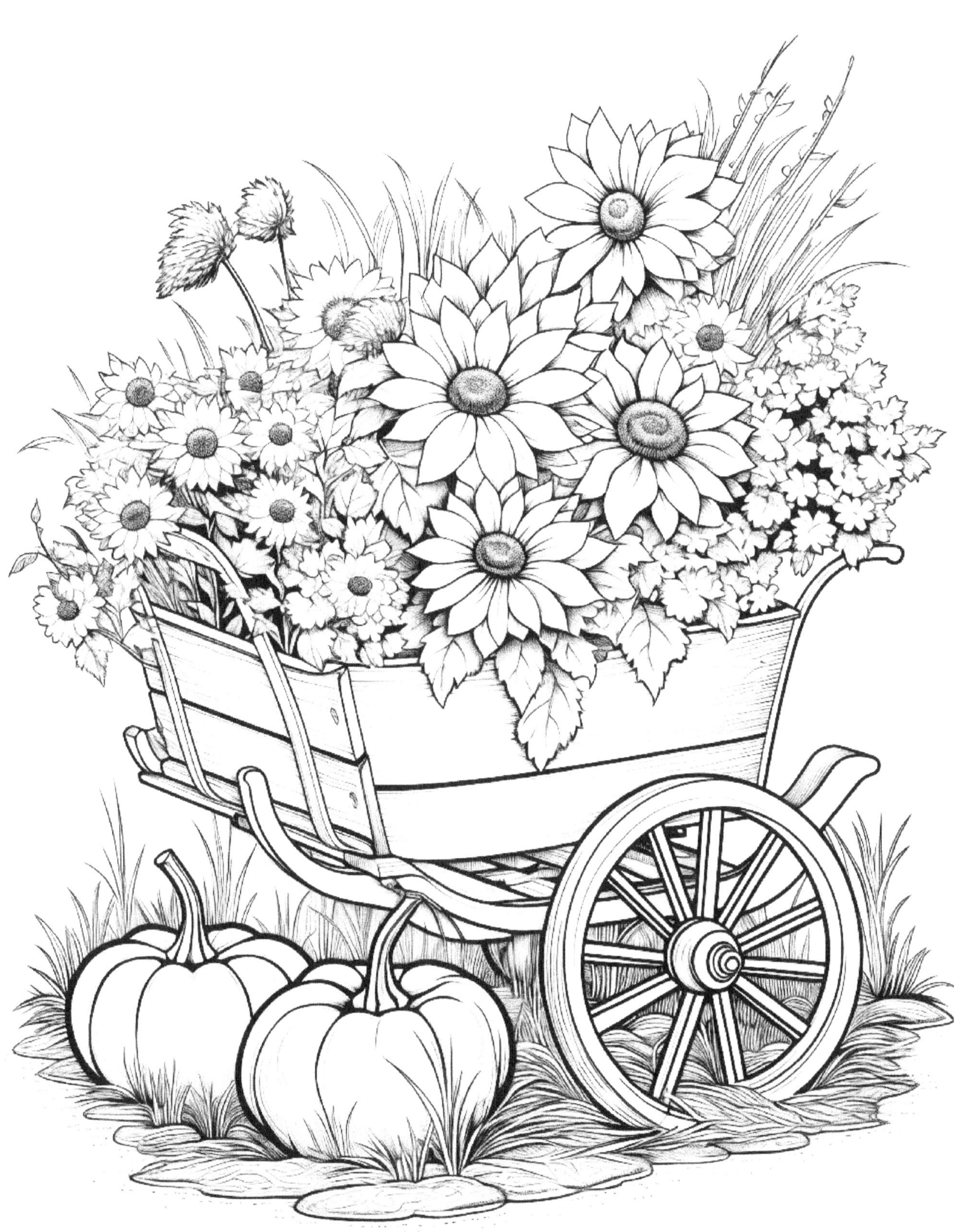

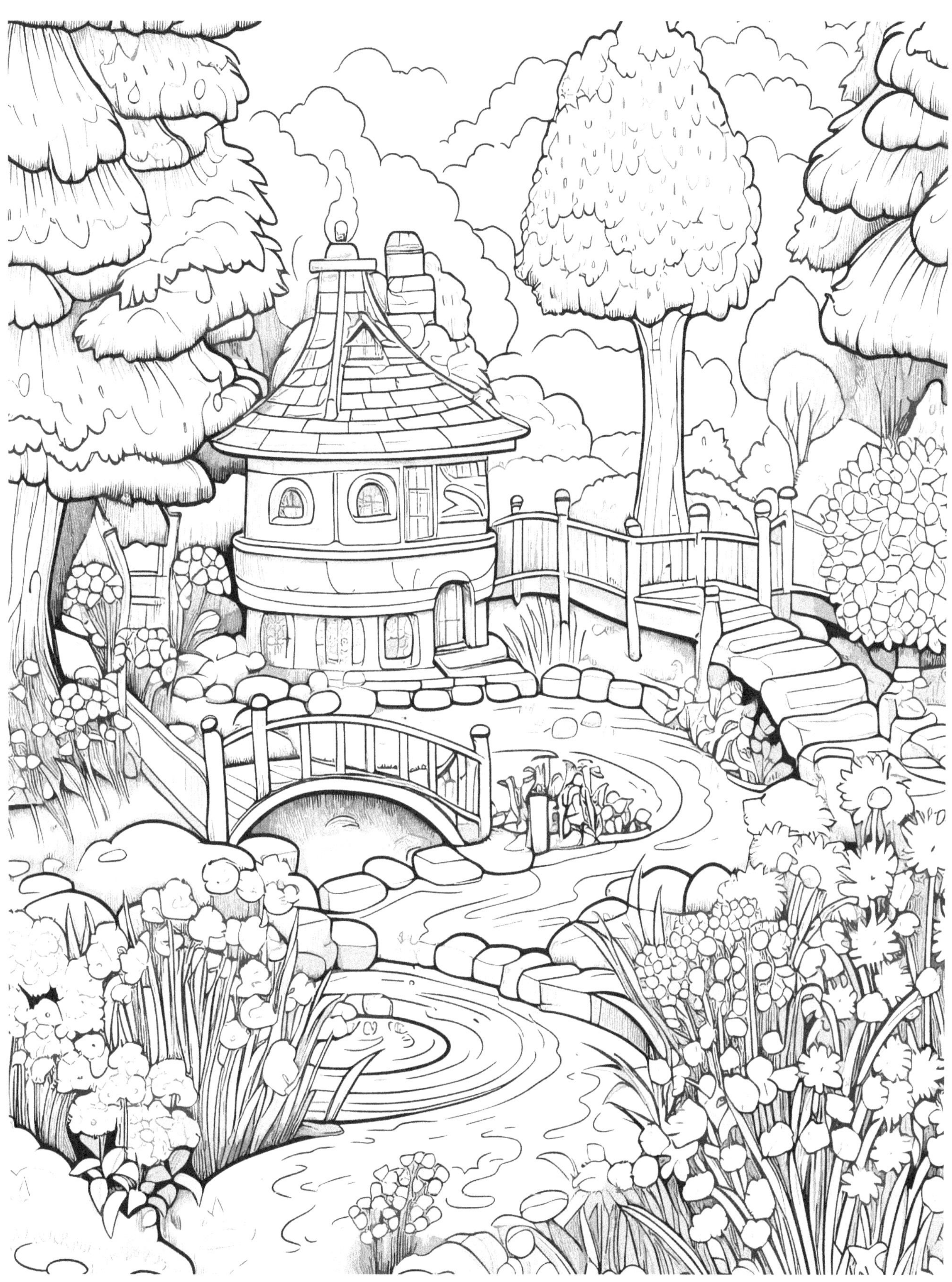

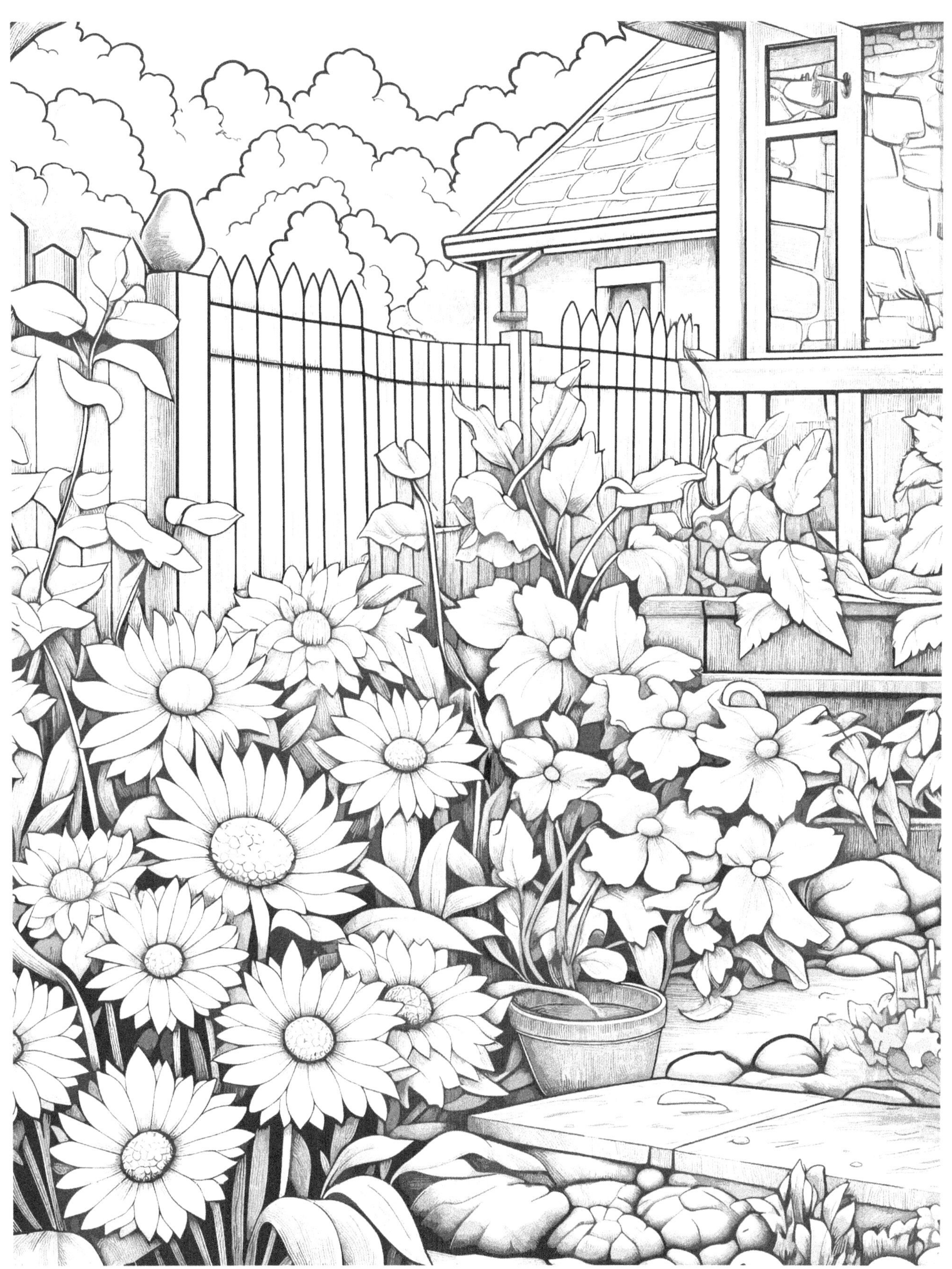

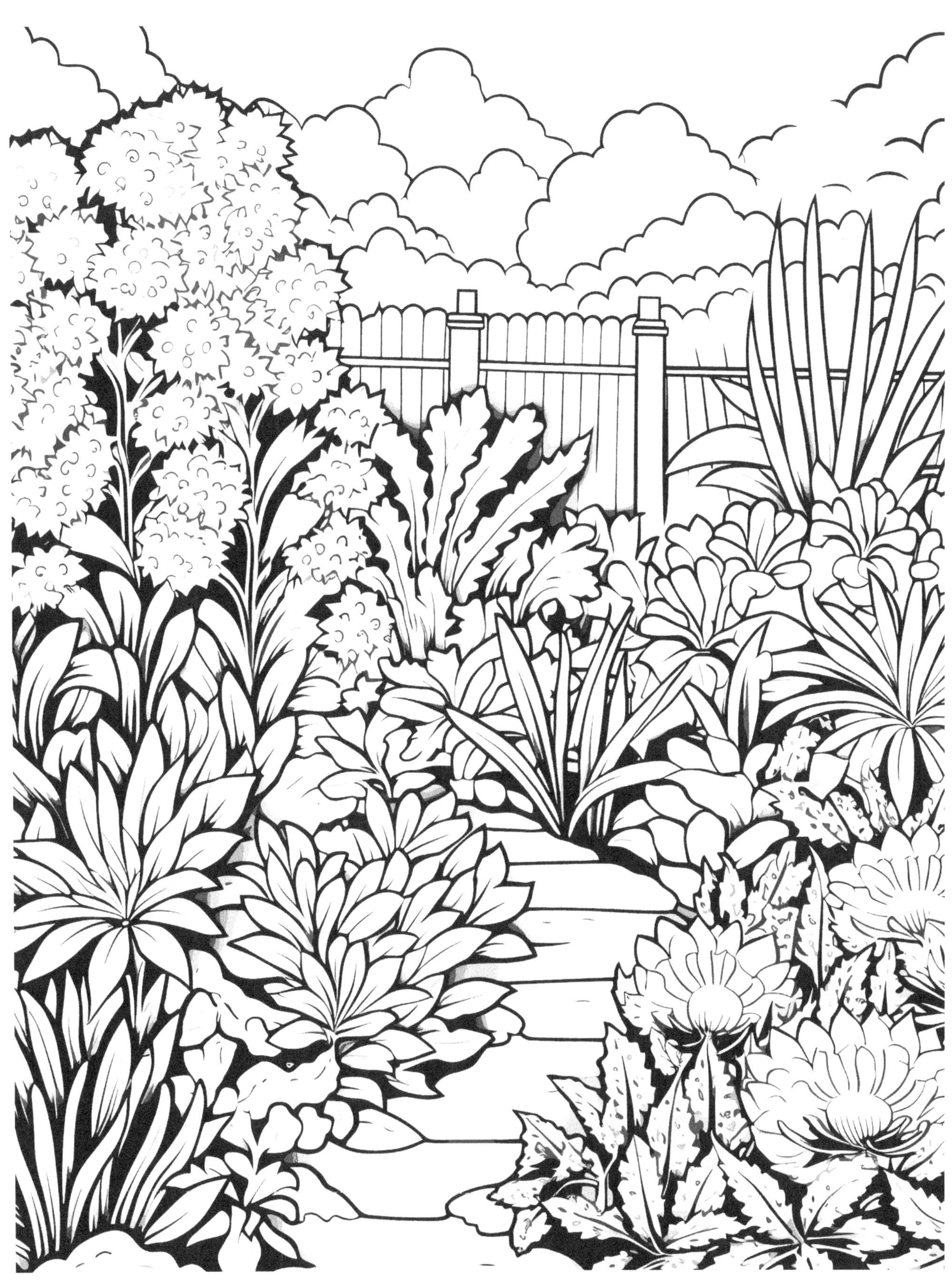

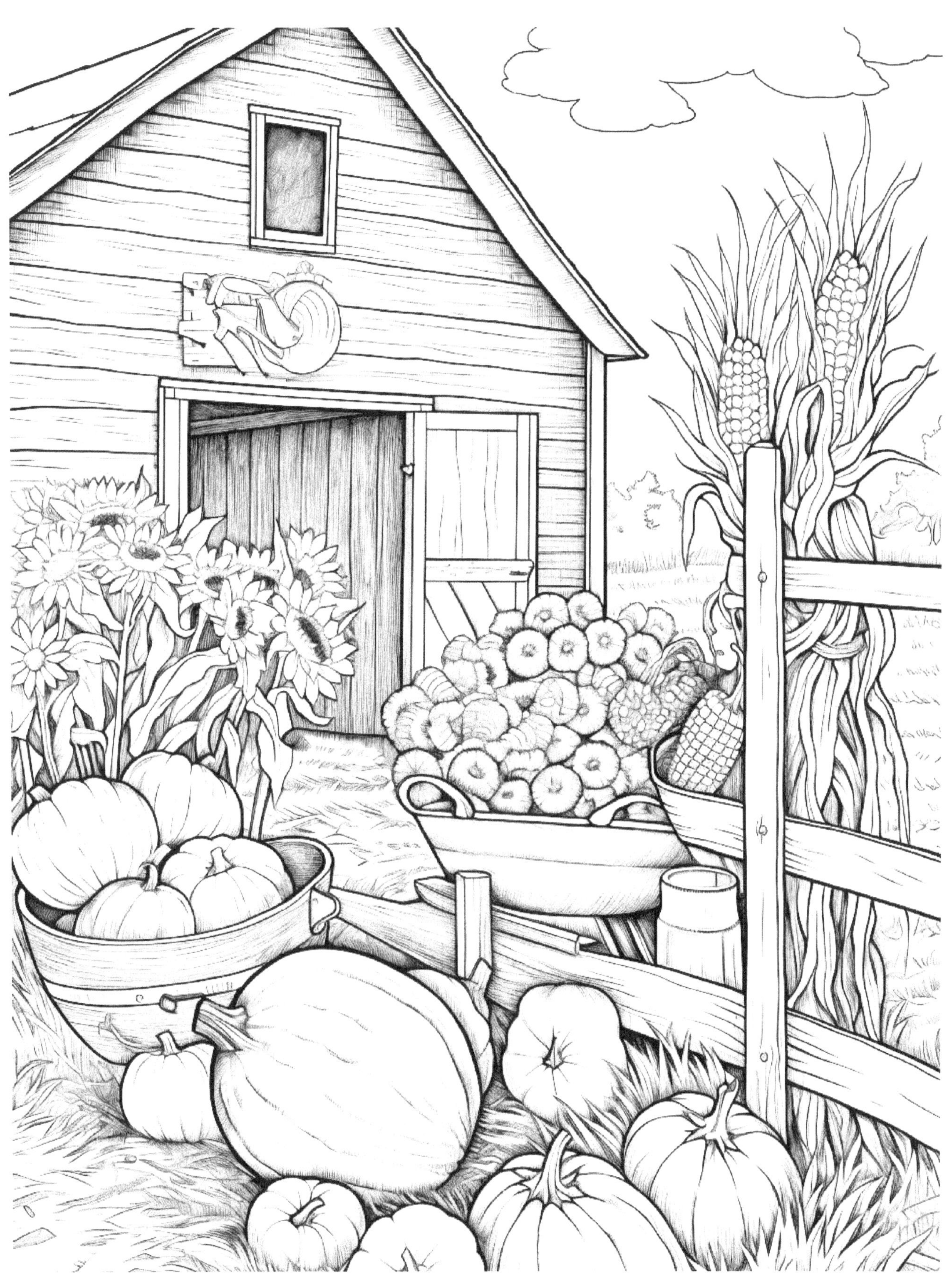